Saving Wildlife

What We've Lost, Saved and are Losing

By
Kenneth Edward Barnes

This book is dedicated to all those that love nature and God's creation.

Contents

Introduction

I was born along the banks of Little Pigeon Creek at the southern tip of Indiana. That was in early April, 1951. I came into the world there at my grandmother's house. Later, when I was four-years old, we moved next door in a small, flat-roofed house that was white with red stripes. Our family always referred to this home as "The Striped House."

We lived here until I was nine, only to move about a half mile away. I was still close enough to fish in Little Pigeon Creek and roam the nearby fields and forests. Since those early childhood days, I have loved nature and wildlife. I loved all of nature and its creatures, but most especially birds. Every bird I saw fascinated me, from the tiny ruby-throated hummingbird to the majestic bald eagle. I loved their color, their songs and their ability to fly.

Abraham Lincoln spent his childhood upstream along Little Pigeon Creek near the small town of Gentryville. I'm sure as a young boy, he fished along its muddy banks just as I did. I grew up near the south end of the creek, just a few miles from where it empties into the mighty Ohio River. With woods and water all around me, there were many birds and animals to see and discover.

As a teenager, I came to know a local celebrity that wrote an outdoor newspaper column and had his own TV segment about the outdoors on a local television station. His name was Joe Celania and he even did television commercials for Evansville businesses.

I also personally knew another local TV celebrity named Marsha Yockey, also known as "The Weather Girl." Marsha read a couple lines from one of my very early works (a children's poem) on her weather forecast in October of 1978. She also mentioned that I wanted to be a writer.

In 1992 I became an outdoor writer for Warrick County Publishing, which published The Boonville Standard and the Newburgh Register. A short time later, I became a member of Hoosier Outdoor Writers. Not long after that I worked for a while at a Fox television station where I wrote, edited, and appeared in wildlife news segments.

After I became an outdoor columnist, I started writing outdoor articles for other newspapers and local magazines. Finally, I got a few nationally published stories in some magazines and one in a hardcover book.

Today I have written over 80 titles, some of which are collections but I do have over 60 novel length books. I write everything from children's books, biblical studies, action-adventure, science fiction, and even pollical commentary. My passion, however, are birds and animals. In this book I have included many of my articles that have been published in newspapers and magazines. These, along with many others about the outdoors, are in my book *Outdoor Adventures*. A few stories in this work are from the first book I ever wrote, which is *Life Along Little Pigeon Creek*. An earlier, slightly shorter version, is titled *Life on Pigeon Creek* and both versions are still available.

This book, however, is mostly about the birds and animals of Indiana, although many of these species live or did live all over North America or in the eastern United States.

Since I was a child, several birds and animals have disappeared from my state of Indiana. The prairie chicken and the ruffed grouse are two birds that are now gone. The swamp rabbit is nearly gone but was common along the Ohio River when I was a child and teenager. The alligator snapping turtle and a giant salamander, the hellbender, are now nearly gone. All of these species I have just mentioned did not die out because of over hunting or poaching, but because of habitat loss. There were many others that disappeared before I was born and I mention them later. A few have been brought back, such as the white-tailed deer, the beaver, wild turkey and otter. Others will never come back because they are extinct.

In this book I have included several stories of the species we have lost and others that have been successfully reintroduced into their former habitat. Nearly all of these stories are articles I've written for newspapers and magazines. Some were written many years ago and in them I made several predictions and every one of them has come true. Therefore, I'm sure that if you love wildlife, there will be many stories in this book that you will enjoy. If so, let me know by going to Amazon and giving it a rating and a book review. Thank you.

Part One:

Conservation Stories:

These next several stories are from my books *Outdoor Adventures* and/or *Barnestorming the Outdoors*. Most of them focus on birds and animals that we've lost, that are rare, or that have made a comeback. These conservation stories were either in my newspaper column or published in several local, regional or national magazines.

Note: The first story, *The Beauty of the Wild*, is from my book *Life Along Little Pigeon Creek*.

Chapter 1

The Beauty of the Wild

Nearly every day I was in the woods and fields, roaming, exploring, and learning new things. I loved the outdoors and all that it contained. I just couldn't get enough of being in the home of all the wild creatures. Besides being in it, I wanted to be a part of it. I wanted to touch it, taste it, and feel it. I liked to feel the wind blowing on me like it did on the tall, stately trees. I wanted to touch it, by being there with it. I also wanted to see it, by searching for all its wonders and secrets. I even wanted to taste it. I loved smelling the air after a summer shower and the flowers in the woods in the spring. Even the smell of the lake and pond had a good smell, like the wilderness itself. When I brought something home, like wild mushrooms, the big turtle, or bullfrogs and ate them, then the wilderness became a part of me and I a part of it. It made me feel kinship with nature and I often felt like one of my heroes, Davy Crockett.

That is why I loved going frog hunting, besides, it let me escape from "the thorn in my side," my little brother, Thomas.

"Mommy, I'm goin' frog hunt'n," I said, as I started out the door with my trusty BB gun in hand.

Walking across the yard and down the hill into the woods, I was thinking about the giant frog I'd seen earlier that week. I had seen the huge frog sitting in the edge of the little pond that was just inside the woods, below our yard, but I hadn't seen him since.

Reaching the pond, I began looking for the big frog, walking very carefully all the way around the pond, but he was nowhere to be found.

"Maybe he has moved to the lake," I thought, so I went up the hill and back farther into the woods to the big lake to try my luck there.

After a while of stalking the edge of the lake without finding him, I gave up and headed back home.

Coming down the last little hill, the pond came back into view. When it did, out of the corner of my eye, to my left, I saw something move.

Stopping, I stood to see something I had never seen before. I looked just in time to see a large, beautiful, snow-white bird, with a long neck and long black legs, leap into the air from a log in the center of the pond.

With the woods surrounding the pond, the white bird contrasted sharply with the green foliage behind him. I watched as the magnificent bird gracefully rose higher and higher into the air, climbing until he cleared the tops of the trees. It then turned in the air and disappeared behind them.

Standing there, I kept staring into the empty blue sky where it had been. Now it seemed like it had never really happened, as if it was only a dream. I had never seen such a beautiful and graceful wild bird. Like a vision, it was there for a few short seconds, then it vanished and was gone forever.

Chapter 2

Photo taken by the author at the St. Lois Zoo.

The Wanderer of Little Pigeon Creek

Passing an old tarpaper covered one-room shack, I walked down a slightly sloping hill. Going a few more steps, I came to a huge sycamore tree that sat on the muddy bank of a stream that was a stone's toss across. The sky was bright blue that mid-October day what little I could see of it, for the tall golden and crimson overhanging maple trees formed a tunnel over the creek making it rather dark. Large patches of sunshine did, however, manage to reach the forest floor here and there.

As I moved passed the sycamore, I was suddenly startled by a mass of green, red and yellow birds that were chattering and screaming as they came rushing from a large hole in the hollow tree just over my head. They were Carolina parakeets and seemed angry that I had disturbed them. The tree evidently was their roosting place. Coming out of the tree, I could see their long tapering tails, pointed wings and their near comical face. The noisy flock of 13 birds flew close together upstream through the tunnel of trees. I stood watching as their brilliant green plumage glistened as they passed through the patches of sunlight that filtered through the trees. I watched until they were out of sight and to where I couldn't hear their vociferous chattering any longer.

"Finally, peace and quiet," I thought. Then taking my seven-foot willow pole, I reached down into the can to retrieve one of the red earthworms. Baiting my hook, I walked to the edge of the water and tossed in the line. After anchoring the end of the pole in the soft mud, I sat back to relax and enjoy the afternoon.

I loved coming here to fish. I was born on its muddy banks in a back room of my grandmother's old three-room house, which sat overlooking the creek.

Sitting there, I heard a loud splash upstream and looked to see a large wave rippling across the water where a big fish had come to the surface. The water was cooler now and fish often seemed to enjoy coming to the surface and showing off.

Turning my attention back to my line, I glanced at the cork bobber, wondering if the huge fish may be coming downstream towards me and my baited hook.

As I thought about how good a platter of golden-brown fish would taste, I heard the unmistakable sound of whirling wings of wood ducks as they were lifting from the water.

Looking downstream, I heard the females uttering their high-pitched call as I saw a flock of perhaps thirty ducks lift into the air. Speeding down the creek, they flew up and over the tops of the trees and were gone. The families that had hatched this year were now gathering, getting ready for their long migration south. "They must have been swimming upstream and seen me." I thought.

Suddenly I saw my cork move, and then it began bobbing up and down as it traveled across the surface of the water. Pulling the pole from the muddy bank, I held it on the ready to set the hook. The cork suddenly disappeared out of sight in the murky water and I yanked on the line.

A large bluegill came up from the depths of the creek and I took hold of the line with my left hand. Carrying the pole and fish to the top of the bank, I removed the hook and picked up a stringer that I had already prepared. After slipping the stick at one end of the stringer through the fish's mouth and gill, I returned it to the water, re-baited my hook, and tossed out the line again.

Sitting there waiting for the next fish to bite, I heard something in the distance. "Was that thunder?" I thought. "It sounds like it, yet it doesn't. It sounded more like a roar."

Standing on the bank listing, it began getting dark. "It must be a storm coming because it's only about 3 o'clock and it won't be getting dark for three or more hours".

The sound then began getting closer and the roar louder. "That's not thunder, but what in the world is it?"

Suddenly the roar became deafening and the sky overhead through the trees looked as if a great shadow was sweeping over it. Looking at the trees, I saw them begin to move. There was no breeze before, but now the wind was picking up and the treetops started moving. I could feel the air moving all around me. "It must be a storm," I thought, "but it can't be." Then a feeling of awe swept over me as the wind picked up with gale force and tears came into my eyes. The trees were now swaying and moving along with everything around me from the great wind. The sky was now so black that I could not see any blue in it.

As the wind moved all around me, it began to rain, but the rain was white! "That's not rain," I thought as it fell on every bush and tree and the ground around me. "It is bird droppings!" I had heard tell of what I was witnessing, but I could not even fathom the awesomeness of the spectacle that was before me.

I could not hear anything but the roaring of millions of wings. I could see the wind moving everything, but the thunderous sound above me was too loud to hear anything else.

Looking to my left, I happen to notice that two men were standing nearby. It was old man Finley and his son Uly from the one room shack. Finley had a double-barreled 12-gauge shotgun and his son had a single-shot of the same gauge. Their pockets were bulging with shells as they raised their guns to fire.

Everything seemed unreal. I saw the blast of the guns and I could see the smoke bellowing from the barrels, but I could not hear them go off, the roaring above me was just too great.

As they continued to fire, it began raining down birds all around me. Some fell motionless and others fell into the creek and began drifting downstream. Some were only wounded and began trying to get up and flutter back into the air to join their comrades passing overhead.

Thousands and then tens of thousands of birds began landing in the trees all along the creek. So many birds filled the limbs of the great trees that even the giant oaks could not take the strain of their weight and began to brake and the limbs and birds came crashing to the ground killing many. Again, I could see the limbs falling but could not hear what I was witnessing.

Looking back at the men, they had stopped shooting, their pockets now empty of the shells but still staring; seemingly mesmerized at the great sight.

A minute or two later, they broke their gaze into the sky and began picking up some of the birds. With both hands full, they tucked their shotguns under their arm and walked up the hill and disappeared.

All around me were still hundreds of dead and wounded birds. Feathers littered the ground, bushes and trees. Blood was sprinkled here and there amongst the white covered forest floor. Birds, feathers and droppings clogged the creek and gently floated downstream. I then looked to see painted-shell turtles gathering at the surface to dine on the bodies of the unfortunate victims.

Standing there, I looked down to see one of the birds on the ground beside me. Reaching down, I picked up its warm limp body. It was a little larger than a mourning dove. It had a long tapering tail like the dove, but its back was bluish gray and its breast pink. It was a male and very handsome. A female lay on the ground just to my left; she was very plain colored, just gray, with some white on her belly and tail. "They must have come from Michigan or Wisconsin," I thought. "That's where their enormous nesting colonies are; their last great stronghold. I've heard that perhaps two billion nests there. I also heard that once there were two or three times as many as there are now. The ones in the east are now nearly gone. Someone told me, too, that the Narragansett Indians called him *Wuskowhan*, which means the wanderer."

I stood in amazement at the sight and sound all around me. It all seemed like a dream and it was, for I was born April 4, 1951, on the banks of Little Pigeon Creek at the southern tip of Indiana. This is several miles downstream from Gentryville, where Abraham Lincoln grew up and near the Ohio River. Now, however, the creek sits empty of its namesake because I was born about one hundred years too late to have seen what I just described. The last passenger pigeon, named Martha, died September 1, 1914 at the Cincinnati Zoo, thus finally and forever ending her species.

As a child, I often wondered why the creek was named so because I never saw a pigeon anywhere near it. Now its muddy banks will never again see the sky darkened with the great migrating flocks that once passed by. Neither I nor my children or grandchildren or will anyone else ever again see one of the greatest spectacles of the world: the wanderer of Little Pigeon Creek.

Chapter 3

This was my first story about the passenger pigeon. It is similar, but different from **The Wanderer of Little Pigeon Creek** and I wanted to include it.

A Living Storm

On April 4, 1951, I was born at my grandmother's house along Little Pigeon Creek in Warrick County, Indiana.

Growing up on the creek in Southern Indiana was good for a little boy. There were newly hatched wood ducks in the spring and baby turtles and frogs to catch. Even a great horned owl nested in a huge sycamore tree on the bank of the creek where my dad and I used to fish. However, as a small child, I often wondered why everyone called it Pigeon Creek; for I never saw pigeons anywhere near it.

Only after I was older, did I learn why it was named as it was, and why there were no pigeons there. When I did learn of the reason it was so named, I was saddened, because at one time, its muddy banks witnessed the greatest numbers of any bird or animal species on earth.

Early in the 1800's, passenger pigeons swarmed over the creek in numbers that cannot even be imagined today. An early naturalist, Alexander Wilson, while traveling between Franklin, Kentucky and the Indiana territory in 1810, saw a flight of passenger pigeons, which he estimated at over 2 billion. Three years later, John James Audubon saw a flight between Louisville and Henderson, Kentucky, which he numbered well over 1 billion.

The passenger pigeon was a beautiful bird, resembling the mourning dove, but being slightly larger. The male had a blue back with a pink breast and a long tapering tail. The female was rather drab like its cousin, the dove.

There were many differences, however. The mourning dove lays two eggs and nests several times a season. The passenger pigeon only laid one egg, and it was believed to have raised just one offspring each year, much like the band-tailed pigeon of our western states. Also like the band-tail, it nested in large flocks. Some of these nesting areas were so large as to stagger the imagination of those who observed them. A nesting colony in Wisconsin was the largest ever found; its size was seventy-five miles long by ten to fifteen miles wide. This nesting area was some seven hundred and fifty square miles, and each tree had dozens of nests in it.

Few, however, ever witnessed these great nesting sites, but in the fall when they began their migration south, it was a different story. The Narragansett Indians called him

Wuskowhan, the wanderer, and part of their scientific name means, the one that migrates.

Like a storm cloud of life, they moved over the land, going south in autumn and north in spring. Traveling at thirty to forty miles an hour, it would often take them days to pass by. The flights would be two miles wide and hundreds of miles long, and so dense that the sun would be darkened as if by a solar eclipse.

When coming to roost, it was said that their wings produced gale force winds and a deafening roar. So loud would be the noise of their beating wings, that if a man fired a shotgun from only a few feet away, it could not be heard.

Large trees where the birds landed to roost in, could often not hold the great weight of their numbers and would come crashing down, killing many of them. Afterwards, when the birds left their roosting area, it appeared as if a tornado had devastated the trees. The forest floor would be white, looking like snow, where two or three inches of their droppings had fallen.

Once they ranged over the entire eastern half of the United States. To the early settlers, they were sometimes a blessing, and at other times, a curse. Swarming into their crops, they would destroy the vital grain. If, however, they arrived after the crops were in, or if the crops had failed, they were an important food supply.

So, what happened to them? How could a creature with numbers so great completely disappear in such a short time?

The Indians had used them as food for centuries. In the East, they often brought young pigeons to the settlements to trade to the pilgrims. However, as the land was cleared and many of their food sources; acorns, beechnuts, and other foods disappeared along with the great forest that they nested in, their numbers began to diminish. This, along with the commercial destruction of their nesting areas was the greatest cause for their decline. For if they had only been shot during their migration, there would be no way that their numbers could have suffered so much, so quickly. One shot could usually bring down only a dozen or so birds, and back in the early 1800's, it was too expensive for the average person to "waste" shells on such small game.

It was the wholesale destruction of their nesting and roosting sights that quickly destroyed them. Their numbers had noticeably decreased in the East by the middle 1800's, and by the 1870's the slaughter began in earnest. In 1875, a wealthy farmer from Ohio, along with hundreds of men invaded a nesting colony in Newaygo County, Michigan. Using nets, which could catch up to 3,000 or more pigeons at a time, and cutting down the trees to obtain squabs, they began the task. The estimated take from this nesting colony was between 40 and 50 *tons* of birds, to be sold to restaurants for one and two cents apiece!

In 1878, another nesting site was found. It was the *last* great nesting colony of passenger pigeons on earth. Within a few weeks, 2,500 men with nets took an unbelievable number of pigeons, which was over one billion one hundred million! A smaller nesting area yielded one million birds in 1881.

By this time, the pigeons were doomed, even though the men with the nets had gone home and there were still thousands left. The few that did remain were still being persecuted, and the last shipment of a handful of birds was received from Arkansas in 1893. Wisconsin saw its last passenger pigeon in 1899, and the last one to fall by man's destruction was killed by a boy in Ohio in March of 1900. After this, none were reported killed. A flock of 200 was seen in Michigan in 1903, and scattered reports continued two or three years later, but by this time there was only one passenger pigeon known to exist on earth. In the Cincinnati, Zoological Garden lived Martha, the last of her kind. Then on September 1, 1914, at 1 o'clock p.m. she died, thus finally and forever ending her species.

So why did the passenger pigeon disappear? Because of greed, and disregard of our responsibility to take care of the earth. If governmental authorities would have passed laws to protect their nesting sites, they still could be with us today.

Did anyone learn anything from the loss of one of God's creatures? Laws were passed a long time later to protect some birds and animals, but only after many were already gone.

In our world today, birds and animals continue to become extinct, and the number one cause is habitat destruction. It seems a shame, and is, that we no longer have the passenger pigeon. Attempts to collect them for breeding came too late. Even if they could have been bred in captivity, it is doubtful they could have existed in the wild. It seems they needed large areas to breed in, and an uninterrupted supply of food on their migration route. With much of the forest destroyed, there were gaps on their journeys and many of their ancestral nesting sites were gone. Only with large areas set aside for them to nest in could they have survived. They also needed large numbers of themselves because of their low reproduction rate.

The band-tailed pigeon nearly had the same fate, but was protected in time. It has since adapted somewhat to man, and is even seen at backyard feeding stations. I would have hoped the passenger pigeon could have adapted too, but we shall never know.

So now, the place I was born sits empty of its namesake. Its muddy banks will never again see the sky darkened with the great flocks that once passed by. I, nor will anyone else ever again see the wanderer of Little Pigeon Creek.

Note: Much of the information about the passenger pigeon in these last two stories, are from a book by Peter Matthiessen. His book was published in 1959. In addition, my son K. Daniel Barnes took the photo at the beginning of this article at the Smithsonian Natural History Museum in Washington DC, USA.

Chapter 4

Forever Lost:
The Carolina Parakeet

In the last one hundred and fifty years, we have lost a host of indigenous birds and animals from North America. A few we have managed to bring back, like the white-tailed deer, the turkey, and the beaver. Others, however, have been gone for so long that many people do not even know they once lived here and will never be brought back because they are extinct. The Labrador duck, sea mink, passenger pigeon and Carolina parakeet are some that are gone forever.

The Carolina parakeet was a beautiful bird that was once common in the eastern half of the United States. A few thick-billed parrots once lived just north of the Mexican border, but disappeared many years ago. An effort was made several years ago to reintroduce them to Arizona, but failed.

Other than this, the Carolina parakeet was the only parrot species to live and nest in the United States.

When our country was first being settled, the Carolina parakeet was very common. This small green parrot, with a yellow and orange head, traveled in noisy flocks and was often seen along the Ohio River where I grew up. They were fond of seeds of the cocklebur weed, and Audubon's famous painting of them, shows several of the parrots in such a bush.

Why aren't they here now?

There are several reasons.

Back in the early days of our country, there were no laws protecting birds or animals. If a person wanted to kill or capture an animal to eat, sell, or just for the sake of killing it, there was nothing to stop them.

One of the reasons they quickly disappeared was because they were very destructive to orchards. Always on the move to find food, they would flock to an orchard and proceed to tear apart the fruit. This habit made them very unpopular with the early settlers who depended on the food they raised to sustain them throughout the year.

A peculiar behavior, however, made them even more susceptible to extinction. While feeding in a tree, all it would take was for one to be shot, and this usually assured the destruction of the entire flock. If the birds would have been frightened and flown away, they may have survived, but they did not. When one of their companions fell, they would fly around overhead squawking and lighting again and again until all were killed. Many parakeets were also killed this way to obtain feathers for women's hats.

Not only were they killed for being destructive to fruit trees and for their beautiful feathers, but many were also captured and sold as pets.

Since the birds were very intelligent and would become tame in only a few days, they were in high demand.

Another behavior of theirs made it very easy to capture them. They roosted in hollow trees, which was one of their downfalls. Because if a person with a gunnysack held the sack over the entrance while someone else struck the tree with a stick, the frightened birds would rush out of the tree into the sack. Thus, would the entire flock be captured.

By the middle of the 1800s, the parakeet's numbers were beginning to dwindle, and they had already disappeared from most of their former range. Once they lived from the East Coast, through the Midwest as far west as Kansas and eastern Texas, and south to Florida. By 1900, only a handful held out in the most remote parts of Florida. It was in this state that the last tiny flock of Carolina parakeets was seen a few years later.

The last Carolina parakeet died in captivity in 1918, at the Cincinnati Zoo according to most authorities. I have also read that it was 1914 or 1920. There was even a claim that a small flock was "rediscovered" in 1930, but all that doesn't really matter, because now the earth is empty of their presence.

In the early 1800s, naturalist Alexander Wilson and Audubon saw them in great numbers along rivers and streams in Kentucky and Southern Indiana where I grew up. Wilson once described how beautiful they were with the sun shining on their brilliant green plumage as a huge flock lifted from the bank of the Ohio River and landed in nearby trees.

I have sometimes sat at my window, in the winter, watching mourning doves flocking to my feeder, alighting in the leafless maple tree above it. I have tried to imagine how it would be if we still had the Carolina parakeet. I could easily picture them in my mind flying across the yard in a small flock and lighting in the tree. Here they would sit, looking down at the tray of sunflower seeds. They would be chattering amongst themselves and pulling themselves up to the next branch with their strong bill as all parrots do today. They would also be "talking" with one another about what they had discovered. I could see their long tapering tails, which were much like the doves, and their brilliant green feathers glistening in the early morning sunshine. Being only about 14 inches long, there would be room for several to be sitting on the feeder while the others were chattering above them in the tree.

If they would have survived to more recent times, with all the modern methods of captive breeding, artificial incubation, and radio transmitters for tracking their movements, they may have been saved. In fact, because of birdhouse erections, backyard-feeding stations, and a different attitude toward wildlife today, they may have made a strong comeback as the wood duck did. They may have even become too numerous and control measures would have had to be taken to protect fruit crops. There probably would be thousands of small flocks throughout the eastern United States. It could have been possible for them to even extend their range as some birds have done due to feeding stations.

This, however, did not happen, and now I can only see them in my mind. I will never see them flocking to a large hollow sycamore tree at dusk along Little Pigeon Creek where I grew up, as they did long ago. I will never see a young one with its all green plumage leaving an old woodpecker hole for its first flight. Not only will I not see them, but also my children will not, nor my children's children. Nor will anyone else.

The woods are a little emptier now, and will never again hear the joyful chattering of our only native North American parrot. For we have lost forever one of God's creations. We have forever lost the Carolina parakeet.

Note: K. Daniel Barnes took the photo at the beginning of this story of the pair of Carolina parakeets also at the Smithsonian Natural History Museum in Washington DC, USA. Below is the famous painting of some Carolina Parakeets on a cocklebur bush by John James Audubon.

Chapter 5

This story was first published in my Warrick County newspaper column in 1993.

The Greatest of Them All:
The Ivory-billed Woodpecker

He was the greatest of his kind in North America. When the colonists first arrived, vast forests covered the eastern half of our nation. And in this virgin timber, lived a giant woodpecker: the ivory-billed. Most plentiful in the South, where cypress trees grew, it haunted the dark forests from where Texas would later be, to Florida and the

Carolinas. They ranged as far north as Illinois and Southern Indiana where I was born.

Northern Indians traveled south to trade for its bill, which was highly prized for ornamentation. Nevertheless, that was long ago. The last confirmed sighting of this great bird in the United States was in 1946, in northern Louisiana.

There are many kinds of woodpeckers in North America, but only one can even be compared to the ivory-billed. The slightly smaller pileated looks similar, but has more black, and the female pileated looks almost identical to the male. The ivory-billed on the other hand, has much more white on it, and the female is nearly all black. Both species have a large red crest, except for the female ivory-billed, which is black. The crow-size pileated's call is a series of high-pitched notes in rapid succession; the ivory-billed's is a single high-pitched one, sounding similar to the white-breasted nuthatch's call of "yank".

What makes the ivory-billed's story so sad, is that it didn't have to come to the verge of extinction. We had already lost the passenger pigeon, Carolina parakeet, Labrador duck, heath hen and sea mink. Others like the Eskimo curlew, whooping crane, trumpeter swan, and bison were also nearly gone. Conservationists tried to halt the destruction of the forest where the woodpeckers lived, but didn't succeed, and the last area where it was certain that they existed was destroyed.

At the time, most people in authority said the woodpecker was already gone and wouldn't do anything to help. There were people who knew they were not extinct and tried to get the government to try to save them, but were ignored.

The ivory-billed woodpecker needs very large tracts of forest to survive. Forest where they feed on insects and grubs under the bark of trees, trees that have been dead for a while. This, however, caused problems for politicians. It cost money to buy large areas of land, and it may offend some who want to cut down all the trees, and this would cost them a few votes. It is much easier to say the bird is extinct and cannot be helped.

But how much is an ivory-billed woodpecker worth? Some would argue that if they can't tolerate the changes that human activity cause, then they should die out. But who are we to push one of God's creations off the face of the earth.

Why can't we live with nature instead of destroying it; for if we destroy nature, we will inevitably destroy ourselves. What right do we have to take away something that can never be replaced; something our descendants will never get to enjoy?

I resent our forefathers for not preserving the passenger pigeon and the other creatures like it. I miss the Carolina parakeet and the Labrador duck. No one had the right to destroy them all.

What is an ivory-billed woodpecker worth? Can a price even be placed on the worth of a species? All the money, time and effort in the world cannot bring them back once they're gone.

Every creature on our planet is worth the time and money to save, if they're in trouble, and to save them while there is still hope. For some day, we too will have to answer to future generations. The questions will be, "Why didn't you save the birds and animals for us to see and enjoy? What right did you have to destroy the things that belonged to everyone?" Not only will we have to answer to future generations, we will have to answer to the Creator who designed and placed them on earth for us to have stewardship over.

Today there is but a tiny glimmer of hope for the ivory-billed. A few were recently discovered in eastern Cuba (an estimated dozen or so) living in a remote mountain forest, a forest that is being cut down. No one knows how long they can hold on, for this was several years ago, now. They are most certainly gone now.

As I write this, there are continued reports of the ivory-billed being sighted in some of our southern states. Nearly every year there are such reports. In most cases, it is probably the pileated woodpecker being seen. There are, however, knowledgeable people who bring in reports every once in a while. Therefore, there still may be a few clinging on to existence in the United States. The glimmer of hope, however, is dimming more each day as the land is cleared and the wild places are growing smaller and smaller.

We can only hope that if there are a few, they will struggle even harder to adapt and live near man, as has their cousin, the pileated. We can also hope that attention is given by everyone to the remaining wild areas that we have left, so they will be protected; thus helping, not only the ivory-billed, but all wildlife.

In our eastern forests, we can see the red-bellied woodpecker, little downy, his bigger cousin the hairy, the yellow-shafted flicker, and the red-headed. In winter, you can find the colorful yellow-bellied sapsucker. Also, in the South, lives a few of the endangered red-cockaded woodpeckers. In places where the woods are large enough, we can still find the impressive pileated. But unless a miracle takes place, you will never see the greatest woodpecker of them all: the ivory-billed.

Footnote: A miracle may have taken place. I wrote an earlier version of this article for my newspaper column in 1993. Recently, as you probably have heard, an Ivory-billed was seen in Louisiana. If they have survived all these years, then there may still be hope for the greatest woodpecker of them all.

Chapter 6

What We've Lost

When America was first discovered by write man, the North American continent teamed with wildlife. Great herds of *Bison* or *Buffalo,* as most knew them, stretched from the Rockies in the west to the Atlantic coast. Their trails crisscrossed the west from Texas through the Great Plains into Canada and all across the Midwest. One trail in Indiana went from east to west just north of where the Interstate 64 highway would later be built.

Mountain Lions, along with *Black Bears* and *Elk* roamed our state, as did the *Gray Wolf. Red Wolves* were also in the southern part of Indiana. In the extreme southwestern tip of the state was the *Spotted Skunk*. In the north, was the *Lynx* and the largest member of the weasel family, the *Wolverine*. His cousin the *Fisher* and its prey the *Porcupine* inhabited the evergreen forest.

White-tailed Deer were everywhere and were an important food source for the Native Americans who lived here. Then there were birds of all kinds. The largest that

roamed Indiana's hills, was the *Eastern Wild Turkey*.
Colorful parrots called the *Carolina Parakeet* were all over
the state. In the southern part of the state, the magnificent
Ivory-billed Woodpecker made its home. The skies were
also filled with a bird that was so numerous that they blotted
out the sun for days as they passed by—the *Passenger
Pigeon*. The great *Bald Eagle* soared in our skies, and the
swiftest of all birds on earth, the *Peregrine Falcon*, hunted
its prey. *Sandhill Cranes* nested in the north, as did the
Whooping Crane and the *Trumpeter Swan*. The *Raven's* call
could also be heard as well as the honking of the giant race
of *Canada Goose*.

Streams were not empty either. *Beavers* were
plentiful, as were *River Otters*. On our prairies, *Prairie
Chickens* did their courting dance and beside them, just
north of where Terre Haute would later be, were a few
Pronghorn Antelope.

Then in less than 157 years from the time Indiana
became a state, and, in most cases, less than 50 years, every
bird and animal I have mentioned was gone. Some like the
Carolina parakeet and passenger pigeon would be lost to the
world forever. And not only were they lost, but others.
There were some American birds and animals that almost no
one even remembers. One was the sea mink that lived along
the North Atlantic coast. Another was the *Heath Hen*, a type
of prairie chicken that lived in the east. The beautiful
Labrador Duck also lived along the East Coast, but
disappeared by 1875. Out in the North Atlantic the *Great
Auk* had already been slaughtered to extinction by the
1840's. A tame flightless bird similar to a penguin about two
feet tall that nested on cold desolate islands was easy prey
for men in ships. On the other side of the continent, in the
North Pacific near Alaska, once swam a giant relative of the
Florida manatee, the *Steller's Sea Cow*. It, too, had been
slaughtered and wiped from the face of the earth by the late
1700's. It also was a victim of man's greed. Just off our cost

in Bermuda, a little petrel called a *Cahow* was slaughtered to extinction because of a famine that hit the island in the 1600's. At least it was thought to be extinct. Then, after nearly 300 years, its call was once again heard, and a handful of individuals were found nesting on a tiny island close by.

One of our most recent birds to be lost has been the Bachman's warbler from our southern states. The *Ivory-billed Woodpecker* like the *Cahow* was thought to have been extinct until one was spotted in Louisiana after having not been seen for 60 years. No new reports have confirmed that they are still alive, however.

Many birds and animals almost went the same way. The *Bald Eagle, Peregrine Falcon, Trumpeter Swan, California Condor*, the tiny *Ross' Goose* and the *Aleutian Goose*, the *Whooping Crane* and the *Eskimo Curlew,* along with many of its cousins of the sandpiper family. Even the *Wood Duck* became rare. Some of the animals that were almost lost were the *Bison, Musk Ox, Red Wolf, Black-footed Ferret, Sea Otter, Elephant Seal* and the American *Crocodile*. The list goes on and on with smaller animals, fish, amphibians, and even insects.

In Indiana, our last *Black Bear* was seen in 1871, the last *Cougar* in 1851. The *Gray Wolf* disappeared in 1908, the last *Red Wolf* in 1832. The last *Bison* and *Elk* faded from our state in 1830. The *Spotted Skunk* was gone by 1920. The *Beaver* was completely trapped out by 1845, and the last of the *Eastern Turkeys* were shot by 1904. The last native *White-tailed Deer* was killed in Knox County in 1893. The *last River Otter* was seen in Posey County at Hovey Lake in 1942 and the last *Prairie Chicken* disappeared from Indiana in 1972.

Others like the *Bobcat* and *Badger* are rare. The *Alligator Snapping Turtle* (the largest fresh water turtle in the world) and the *Swamp Rabbit,* both of which inhabit the southwestern tip of the state, are also rare. The *Swamp*

Rabbit, which lives in only a few counties along the Ohio and Wabash Rivers, has nearly disappeared because of habitat destruction.

I could go on with the list of smaller animals; fish and reptiles that are gone or endangered like the largest salamander in North America, the *Hellbender*, which lives in only a few of the rivers in the southern tip of Indiana.

Some birds and animals have been brought back to Indiana like the White-tailed *Deer, Turkey, Beaver, Bald Eagle, Peregrine Falcon*, and most recently, the *Otter*. The *Bobcat* and *Badger* have begun to increase and some birds have begun nesting here again, the *Sandhill Crane* is one, but others will never again inhabit our state because their habitat is gone and cannot be restored.

Not only species, but also many races of birds and animals in North America are gone forever. The *Eastern Elk*, the *Plains Grizzly*, the *Badlands Bighorn Sheep* and the *Dusky Seaside Sparrow* are a few that are now only history.

These are just the animals in North America; worldwide wildlife has disappeared and is now disappearing at an even faster rate. Tasmania lost its largest marsupial predator the *Tasmanian Wolf* or *Tasmanian Tiger* as some call it. The most famous and one of the first creatures to disappear because of man was the flightless *Dodo* bird. Not long afterwards, the largest of all birds, the *Giant Moa* and the *Elephant Bird* were added to the list.

What will happen if things continue as they are? As the fabric of our planet is torn away piece by piece, the land, air and water polluted and destroyed, along with its creatures, we too will go the way of the dodo and others like it. This planet can only take so much destruction and it too will get rid of the *"disease"* that is causing its suffering. We are like a modern-day Noah, able to save what is here if we choose to or stand by and watch our world die all around us. If our past is any indication of our future, only *God Almighty* will be able to save our world and us.

Photo was taken by permission of M.R. James, author of "Hunting the Dream"

An update: The ruffed grouse, pictured above, is probably gone from Indiana. None have been seen for several years. They were getting more common after the 1930's, when many Hoosier farms became abandoned during the Great Depression. Now, because of habitat loss over the last thirty years, they have disappeared. It seems a shame that Indiana sportsmen have spent millions of dollars for licenses, habitat stamps and taxes on sporting goods to help game management; then, the ones in authority, the ones that are supposed to guard our birds and animals, lets a marvelous bird such as the ruffed grouse slip into oblivion.

Chapter 7

This article was first written July 27, 1994 in my column of the Boonville Standard.

There's Hope for Bobcats

In the summer of 1963, I was 12 years old and one of the things I enjoyed doing the most was fishing. It didn't matter where, as long as I had a chance to catch a fish, turtle, or even a crawfish. This particular day I decided to go down an old dirt road that was behind our house that ran to the Ohio River. A short distance down this road was a small ditch that ran from a swamp about a half-mile away. The little stream flowed under the road and then continued on to the river, which was about another half-mile away. Where this ditch went under the road, there was a concrete culvert and where the water came out, it was wider and deeper than any other place along the ditch. It was a perfect spot to try my luck at catching something.

After baiting my hook and tossing my line in, I stuck the end of the cane pole in the ground and sat back to wait for a bite. I guess it was only five or ten minutes later that I heard a kitten meowing across the ditch in a thicket. "Someone's kitten must be lost," I thought. I reasoned this because there was a house just on the other side of the thicket and a short distance up the hill, probably no more than three hundred feet from where I sat.

As I sat there listening to the poor little kitten crying, I decided I would go and find it, (as soon as I fished a little more). A couple of minutes later, however, I happened to glance up the road. Sitting down the bank, close to the water, I was about eye-level with the road. Suddenly my serenity ended, because to my surprise, a large spotted cat with pointed ears and a short tail trotted across the dusty road not 40 feet away. It was heading towards the thicket.

Quickly gathering up my line and using the pole in front of me as a weapon, in case the big cat came back out, I ended my fishing trip and ran home.

This was the first and last time I saw one of Indiana's most endangered animals. I did get a glimpse of what I thought was a bobcat when I was about six or seven years old while riding the bus to school one day. As we passed an old "slack road" near Little Pigeon Creek, I looked down the road and saw an animal standing in the road and it looked back at the bus as we passed. It looked as if it had pointed ears and looked like a cat to me, so I believe it was a bobcat, but I can't be sure.

In May of 1989, the Indiana Bobcat Report Database was established to analyze reports of bobcats throughout the state. The database (as of 1991) had 134 unconfirmed bobcat sightings. There have been only seven confirmed reports in 21 years. One of those was in 1990, in northeast Warrick County, where one was killed on Interstate 64.

After an examination, it was revealed that the bobcat was a female and she had bred the year before.

Of course, there are several sightings a year that go unreported. If you do see one, report it to a local Conservation Officer and he can relay the information to the Division of Fish and Wildlife. By no means, harm it, not only because it is against the law, but they are a native species that is barely hanging on to existence in our state.

Out west, the bobcat is very common. Here they have abundant prey such as jackrabbits, and have plenty of wide-open spaces to hunt. In the Midwest, the forests have been cut down and they must compete with a host of other predators. Not only do they have to contend with foxes, owls and hawks, which are native species, but with man and his animals. Dogs and cats not only disrupt and disturb wildlife; they also destroy many birds and animals. Now the bobcat must compete with a new arrival, the coyote. Therefore, with the limited amount of space and competition they are having a difficult time surviving.

What are the future prospects for Indiana's bobcats? In the past, they were persecuted and destroyed whenever found. They were seen as a competitor for game birds and animals, and as one who killed livestock.

Bobcats are very shy and secretive and almost never seen in the daytime. An Indiana bobcat scent station survey done in 1990 shows how difficult it is to find them. In a ten-county area from May to November, 955 operable station-nights were recorded from 16 survey routes and no bobcat tracks were identified. From all the data (2,634 operable station-nights) only one confirmed bobcat visitation occurred.

Even when bobcats are common they are not often seen, and when they are nearly extinct, it is a very rare occurrence to see one. Recently (1994) I began working at Allied Sporting Goods, in Evansville, in the hunting and fishing department. We have a mounted bobcat specimen and it attracts a lot of attention and because of it, I sometimes receive information on local bobcat sightings. One gentleman told me of a sighting he had of a young bobcat on a farm in Kentucky last summer (they are uncommon, but not so rare in Kentucky). Another gentleman from Warrick County, in Indiana, told me of a bobcat that tried to climb the tree he had his deer stand in. He said it began climbing the tree until it looked up and saw him, then quietly climbed back down and left.

There is hope for bobcats, but it will take effort on everyone's part. You can buy Game Bird Habitat stamps, duck stamps, or donate money by using the Nongame Tax Check off when you fill out your tax papers. When land is improved for game birds and animals such as grouse, turkey, rabbits or ducks, all birds and animals benefit; game and nongame alike. We can also keep our dogs and cats from roaming the woods and fields, especially in the spring when birds and animals are having their young. We can plant trees and let certain areas grow up for wildlife. We can also educate our young people on the value of nature and wildlife. We need to do all we can so we will not lose the rarest of Indiana's predators: the bobcat.

Update: In the late summer of 2010, my wife Elizabeth and I were driving in Dubois County, close to the town of Ferdinand, and got a glimpse of a bobcat. It was sitting on a bank next to the road, but we did not see it until it turned and jumped into the weeds. We both got a good look at its tail as it disappeared and we both said, "What was that!" I said it out of surprise for I knew instantly what it was because no other animal has a short tail with the color and size of the bobcat. That same winter, I was proved right, for a farmer caught two male bobcats within a few hundred yards of that very spot.

Every year since the mid-nineties, bobcat numbers have been climbing and road kills are becoming more and more common. It seems they have adapted somewhat to man, first in the west and now in the Midwest. So, don't be surprised if someday you encounter a fascinating creature that is part of our natural world: the bobcat.

A later update: In 2013, my son David told me that he had seen a bobcat in a forest that was within a quarter mile of where I saw the one when I was a kid. This past year, 2014, a neighbor told me that a friend of his saw a bobcat early one morning run across the road. The bobcat had been on my property! Then just as the new year of 2015 began, my next-door neighbor had a bobcat sitting in his yard watching his house. He took a photo of it with his cell phone. Most likely, this was the one that was on my property earlier, so they are back.

A bobcat caught on a trail camera in my backyard!

Chapter 8

Above is a cougar owned by a relative. This story first appeared July 13, 1994 in my column of the Boonville Standard.

The Cougar Could Return

The beaver is already gone, so is the buffalo, elk, red wolf, and Indiana's last bear was killed the year before. The year is 1851, and the last cougar is roaming the forest of Indiana.

In the early days, the rolling hills of the state had many as he, but that was 50 years before. When the pioneers first came into Indiana's territory, they often had scouts go ahead of the wagons to look for mountain lions. The large cats had the habit of lying on limbs on large trees over the trails where they watched for game to come by. Many of the trails the pioneers followed were in fact game trails. One such trail was the Buffalo Trail that ran just north of what would later be Interstate Highway 64. The evidence of this path the buffalo followed can still be seen in some places.

The large brown cat, which can weigh up to 296 pounds (record weight), is known by many names; cougar, mountain lion, puma, panther, and several others. His chief prey is the white-tailed deer. With the clearing of the land, the disappearance of the deer, and the relentless persecution, the cats became increasingly rare. All throughout the East, Midwest, and South, their numbers fell. By 1880, they were gone from Vermont and New Hampshire. New York State paid a bounty on 107 cougars in 1890. The last one in the Northeast was recorded in 1903, in the Adirondacks. Shortly thereafter, they were gone from the Appalachians. The only known Eastern cougars were a tiny population living in the Florida Everglades.

Several decades passed and it seemed the Eastern mountain lion was extinct, or soon would be when the small population in Florida died out. Then came evidence that there were cougars surviving in the Canadian province of New Brunswick. In 1969, five park workers in the Great Smokey Mountain National Park saw what they believed to be a cougar chasing a deer. Reports of cougar sightings continued, but now in several regions. Maine, New York, New Hampshire, Vermont, Virginia, West Virginia, Massachusetts, South Carolina, North Carolina, Georgia, Louisiana, Alabama, Arkansas, Mississippi, Tennessee, and Missouri all reported sightings of cougars. Then there were two unconfirmed sightings in Michigan.

How could an animal thought not exist, hide undetected for so long? The leopard of the Middle East was thought to be extinct. Then in 1969, one was found living in Jordan. Since that time, several others have been found. Cats of all species are very secretive and elusive. In addition, when they have been hunted for many years they become even more so.

With many wilderness areas set aside, the reintroduction of their main food source (the white-tailed deer) and protection, they have begun to increase.

The cougar is a very efficient predator, being able to catch and kill its prey 80 percent of the time. An African lion is successful in only one out of ten tries. Besides deer, it will prey on nearly anything small enough to kill. Turkeys, rabbits, porcupines, and beaver are killed when the opportunity arises. They can eat around ten pounds of meat per day and if there is any left, they will cover it up with leaves and other debris to hide it. They will keep coming back to the carcass to feed until it's gone or begins to spoil.

They also hunt in a large territory. The males live in an area of up to 50 or 60 square miles; the female's is considerably smaller. Often, they travel 20 or more miles a day in their search for food. Usually they avoid livestock, but once they learn domestic animals are an easy meal the individual will continue killing until it is destroyed. One cougar was known to have killed over 190 sheep in one night.

The cougar does not roar, but squalls during mating season and the sound can be very unnerving to anyone unfamiliar with its call. The kittens are very cute, having a spotted coat and blue eyes when young.

What good is a predator such as the cougar? They are an intricate part of the balance of nature. They are a natural control measure on the population of deer and other animals.

The wolf once shared in this role, but is now gone from most of its former range. It was more conspicuous because it hunted in packs and was very vocal. For these reasons, it was easier to wipe out. The cat, being shy and hunting alone was not as easily found.

But is there room for the cougar? Deer have multiplied to, in some places an overabundance. And it will not hurt sportsmen to share a few to support a small number of cats. The habitat being so reduced it cannot support many of the cougars anyway. Every creature deserves a place to live and the cougar is a native who is again bringing back a little of the wilderness to America.

Update: Since the time I first wrote this article, there have been a rash of confirmed sightings of cougars in several states where they were once totally absent. They have been seen alive or found dead on roadways in Missouri, Michigan and Illinois. Then on May 1, 2010, a cougar sighting was confirmed in Greene County, Indiana by a photo taken on a trail camera. Other evidence also was found nearby and other sightings have been reported not far away (probably the same animal). So, my prediction of the return of the cougar has proved true.

Garden of the Gods in Southern Illinois where a cougar returned, only to be killed.

Chapter 9

First published in my column of the Perry County News, January 12, 1995.

Could Black Bears Return to Indiana?

Martin Luther Vanada was born near Newburgh, Indiana, December 4, 1815. According to a May 25, 1909 *Evansville Courier* article, he, as a young man, killed a bear within a hundred yards of his home in Warrick County. This must have been in the mid to late 1830's for by 1850 black bears were gone from Indiana.

In the early settlement of our state, bears were very plentiful and were a valuable food source to the pioneers. Not only was their flesh eaten, but their skins made warm covering on cold nights. It has been said that as a child, Abraham Lincoln used a bearskin for this purpose; their fat was also used, by being made into grease.

Besides being valuable, bears were often destructive to livestock. Back in those days, many people let their hogs run free in the forest to fend for themselves on acorns, or whatever they could find. Bears would often make a quick and easy meal of the pigs.

This did not make the settlers happy and the bear was looked upon as an animal to be destroyed whenever and wherever found. After several decades of unregulated hunting and forest destruction black bears died out.

The same thing happened in other Midwestern states. Ohio's last known bear was killed in Paulding County, in 1881. They were also killed out in Illinois and Kentucky. By the early 1900's their numbers in other Midwestern and southern states were low or nonexistent.

The persecution continued until the 1950's. It was about this time that they were seen as a valuable game animal and protected. Arkansas had a small population, but the state (the only one to do so up to this time) brought in bears from Wisconsin for release to try to build up their numbers. It worked and their population began to rise. Soon bears were being seen in Missouri.

With protection, bear populations in other states also started to rebound. In the last several years, bears have moved into Kentucky from West Virginia, Virginia and Tennessee. They were thought to be gone from Kentucky by 1900, but occasional reports of sightings in remote parts of the Cumberland Plateau continued through the 1970's.

Then documented sightings in the early 1980's increased until today. Reliable reports are now being received from many eastern Kentucky counties, so it is definite; black bears are back in Kentucky.

The same thing has happened in Ohio. Several years ago, they were reported being seen swimming the Ohio River from West Virginia. In the early 1970's biologists were receiving reports of bears being seen in Ohio counties bordering Pennsylvania.

What happens when bears come to an area where they haven't been seen for decades? Often, frightened people kill them. In areas where people have never seen one, a bear can be very startling. In some states, where they are common, people and bears get along well and seeing one is not such a shock. In Pennsylvania, bears sometimes come to backyard bird feeding stations. They have even been known to sleep the winter months under the floor of an occupied home.

When bears first began showing up in new areas, one man in Ohio was hunting groundhogs when a bear came out of the woods near him. After killing the bear, he claimed self-defense, but was cited on charges of taking a bear out of season.

I received information that two bears were released in the Shawnee National Forest in Illinois; one was soon shot and the other hit by a car. I also have reliable information that a few bears exist or occasionally wander into the southern part of Illinois from Missouri.

So, what are the prospects for bears one day returning to Indiana? Indiana is one of the few states that do not have any bears. Only South Dakota, Delaware, Rhode Island, Iowa, Illinois and Indiana are not supposed to have bears. This information comes from an article written in 1981. It also mentions Ohio as not having any, but this of course has changed.

It also seems logical that, if things continue as they are, in several decades a few bears could show up in the southern part of our state, most likely in the Hoosier National Forest. Being of very limited habitat, few bears could survive. I have, however, heard reports of bear sightings in Indiana, and anything is possible.

Sever years ago, a farmer in Iowa was harvesting a wheat field when he hit a 250-pound female black bear with his combine. She was curled up asleep in his field. Bears are not supposed to be in Iowa!

Bears often travel waterways and have been known to travel a hundred miles or more after being relocated and returning to the area where they had been captured.

Black bears are large animals. One killed in Wisconsin weighed over 800-pounds. Since they are large and powerful and have teeth and claws, bears can be dangerous, and there are many cases of black bears killing and mauling humans.

Usually, however, they are shy, try to stay away from people, and are not often seen, even in areas where they are common. However, once they get over their shyness, bears can become a nuisance.

One in Ohio got in the habit of raiding a dumpster that contained the remains of ice-cream containers and cake frosting. After the bear was trapped, tagged and transported to a more remote part of Ohio, it was hoped that the shock of capture would break him of his bad behavior. Six days later, however, conservation officers in Kentucky, shot the bear after it was seen raiding a dumpster at a restaurant near the Ohio River.

The black bear is like many animals that have benefited from protection and the preservation of areas where they can live. Because of this, they are responding by moving back into places that haven't seen them for more than a century. The population in the lower 48 states is an estimated 160,000 (1981 figures). Therefore, maybe someday we will again see black bears roaming the hills of Indiana.

Update: In the fall of 2010, I read an article by a fellow outdoor writer who said there have been unconfirmed reports of bears seen in Indiana. I predicted the rise in population of the bobcat. I predicted the possible return of the cougar, which has happened. Since this article was first written in 1995, bears are becoming more common in Kentucky, Ohio and have just returned to Illinois. I remember when I wrote this article and displayed it at the sporting goods store where I worked, someone wrote across the top of the page, "Ya right"! I suppose they thought it would be impossible for bears to return to Indiana. If a cougar, which was thought to be extinct east of the Mississippi could show up here, it is very likely, that given enough time, a bear will follow. If justice is served, this gentleman that made fun of my story will be the first to meet a black bear in Indiana. Maybe it will be a close encounter (hopefully not of the third kind) then we all will have the last laugh.

Black bears could return to Indiana

Martin Luther Vanada was born near Newburgh Dec. 4, 1815. According to a May 25, 1909 *Evansville Courier* article, he, as a young man, killed a bear within a hundred yards of his home in Warrick County. This must have been in the mid to late 1830s, for by 1850 black bears were gone from Indiana.

In the early settlement of our state, bears were very plentiful and were a valuable food source to the pioneers. Not only was their flesh eaten, but their skins made warm covering on cold nights (it's said that, as a child, Abraham Lincoln used a bear skin for this purpose). The fat was also used by being made into bear grease.

But besides being valuable, bears were often destructive to livestock. Back in those days, many people let their hogs run free in the forest to fend for themselves on acorns or whatever they could find. Bears would often make a quick and easy meal of the pigs.

This didn't make the settlers happy and the bear was looked

KENNY BARNES
OUTDOORS COLUMNIST

numbers. It worked, and their population began to rise. Soon bears were being seen in Missouri.

With protection, bear populations in other states also started to rebound. In the last several years, bears have moved into Kentucky from West Virginia, Virginia and Tennessee. They were thought to be gone from the state by 1900, but occasional reports of sightings in remote parts of the Cumberland Plateau continued through the 1970s.

Then documented sightings in the early '80s increased until today. Reliable reports are now being come to backyard bird feeding stations; they have even been known to sleep the winter months under the floor of an occupied home.

One man in Ohio was hunting groundhogs when a bear came out of the woods near him. After killing the bear, he claimed self-defense, but was cited on charges of taking a bear out of season.

I received information that two bears were released in the Shawnee Nation Forest in Illinois; one was soon shot and the other hit by a car. I also have reliable information that a few bears exist, or occasionally wander into the southern part of Illinois from Missouri.

So, what are the prospects for bears one day returning to Indiana? Indiana is one of the few states that do not have any bears. Only South Dakota, Delaware, Rhode Island, Iowa and Illinois are not supposed to have bears. This information comes from an article written in 1981; it also mentioned Ohio as not having any, but this, of course, has changed.

It also seems logical that, if things continue as they are, in sev- a tea kettle. If it was a bear, I don't know why, or how, it got there. But I do remember the tracks very well—they had three-inch claw marks protruding from them.

Bears often travel waterways and have been known to travel a hundred miles or so after returning to an area where they had been captured and relocated.

Black bears are large animals. One killed in Wisconsin weighed over 800 pounds. The world record is over 900 pounds for one in Arizona. Since they are large, and have teeth and claws, bears can be dangerous, and there are many cases of black bears killing humans.

Usually, however, they're shy and try to stay away from people, and are not often seen, even in areas where they are common. But once they get over their shyness, bears can become a nuisance.

One in Ohio got in the habit of raiding a dumpster that contained the remains of ice cream containers and cake frosting. After being trapped, tagged and transported to a

51

Chapter 10

Mounted bear above is a Kentucky black bear at Kingdom Come State Park.

Indiana Black Bears

Back in 1995, I wrote several articles in my newspaper columns about the disappearance of many of our native birds and animals. One was about the cougar and the other was about black bears. I said in both, that if things continue as they have, it would only be a matter of time until the cougar and black bear could return to Indiana. The cougar disappeared in 1851, and it indeed found its way back just a few years ago. It is not yet breeding, but give it time. The black bear has not yet returned, but just across the Ohio River, they have been seen in central and north central

Kentucky, near Owensboro. The only thing stopping them from reaching Indiana is a short swim across the river.

This past Labor Day (2013), my wife Lilly and I visited some of her relatives in Eastern Kentucky, in Perry County. This area is in the middle of the range of Kentucky's elk herd and where black bears first showed up many years ago. The bear is now very common there and even a nuisance. We went there last year also, but I was not lucky enough to see a bear. We even went driving around at night hoping to see one, but didn't even get a glimpse. We did find out later, that only a half mile from the house where we were staying, a bear had raided a neighbor's garbage can that very night.

Lilly's cousin on the mountainside, just above where we were, often has black bears tearing up her bird feeders and stealing bags of dog food from the back of their pick-up truck. Lilly's aunt that lives across the road from her cousin, has had bears come into the carport and attempt to open an old, up-right freezer where dog food is stored. Muddy paw prints were left behind along with dents in the freezer to show the bear's frustration at not being able to get to the food. This past year, after storing the dog food elsewhere, the bears knocked over the freezer to try to open it with the hope there was still something inside for them to eat. The bears have also torn down her humming bird feeders on the front porch. She even saw one looking in her living room window early one morning.

While visiting Cumberland, KY, Lilly and I went to Kingdom Come State Park, which is only a few miles from where we were staying. They have bear crossing signs posted and a gift shop near a lake. Inside the gift shop, they have a black bear on display that was recently mounted. The bear was hit by a vehicle while trying to cross a major highway just a few miles away.

I do not know if black bears will show up in Indiana in my lifetime, but if there is still some habitat left and they continue to increase in Kentucky, it is only a matter of time before there will once again be Indiana black bears.

An update: According to a comment on the Internet, a black bear was sighted in the northwestern part of Indiana on April 20, 2012, at 1:05 pm on I-65 at the 220-mile marker. The gentleman, Bob Haskin, who saw it, said that he got a good look at the bear as it ran across an open area. He also said that he and several cars pulled over to see the bear. The bear was later seen and killed by the Department of Natural Resources because "it was a problem bear."

Then in 2015, another credible sighting of a black bear was reported in northern Indiana. Evidently, they have wondered in from Michigan.

A third sighting was in July of 2016, when a black bear was seen and photographed near the town of Corydon in southeastern Indiana. In addition, in 2019, a fourth bear was hit by a car near New Albany, wondered off injured but was never found. These was the first confirmed sightings since 1871!

Chapter 11

Photo was taken by the author by permission of M. R. James, author of "Hunting the Dream."

Indiana Elk

Recently I traveled to southeastern Kentucky, in Perry County, where my wife has relatives for their annual family reunion. We stayed at her aunt's home over the Labor Day weekend where on more than one occasion black bears have peeked into her living room window or took a snooze in her front yard. I was hoping to see one, but after four such tips, I didn't even get a glimpse of one. The same goes for Kentucky's elk. Though they now roam south eastern Kentucky in numbers of around 10,000, I failed to see even one. Others that came to the reunion did see a bear and an elk.

Kentucky has the largest population of elk east of the Mississippi River and they are confined to only 16 counties. Not only do they have the most elk, the elk are larger on average by 15 percent than the ones out west. The population has soared in the last twenty years because of plenty of food and no natural predators.

The eastern elk disappeared from Indiana sometime during the 1840s. The last elk in the east was reportedly killed in Pennsylvania in 1867 ironically by a Native American named Jim Jacobs. This fact was in an old book by Peter Matthiessen titled Wildlife in America. The copyright for the book was issued in 1959. Since that book was written many animals have made a comeback in America: The white-tailed deer, the beaver, the river otter, and the turkey to name a few. Perhaps someday we could add the elk to that list.

If you have ever been in eastern Kentucky, near the Virginia border, it is amazing that any game animal that must walk could live there. The mountains are so steep that it would seem to be very difficult for deer, bear or elk to climb them. Most do have trails where they travel less difficult terrain. Indiana would have much better topography and even more food for elk if they were present. Sadly, the only elk found in Indiana are on farms that raise them. There was a farm near my home in Perry County several years ago and now there is one near the city of Jasper in Dubois County. I have eaten elk meat from that farm when it was sold in a nearby grocery store.

Many eastern states have small populations of elk and I see no reason Indiana couldn't have a few. The Hoosier National Forest stretches a long way in the southern part of the state. In and around the national forest are thousands of acres of State Forest also, not to mention private land.

The elk makes a white-tailed deer look tiny. A large bull elk can stand over five feet high at the shoulder and tip the scales at 1,100 pounds. During the rut, the males have an ear-piercing bugle call that echoes through the forest that they claim for their territory. The dominate bulls have harems of several females and will sometime fight to the death defending them from rival males.

Kentucky's elk herd has grown so much that there has been an open season now for several years. There is also an archery season besides a firearms season. A .270 caliber rifle or larger must be used to hunt them and some real trophies have already been taken. Each year there is a quote set and it is not easy to draw a permit to hunt them. Some hunters have tried since the season first began without drawing one. Nonresidents can also get in on the action, but it takes a lot of money for the nonresident hunting license, the elk permit, and the application permit. That is if you are lucky enough to have your name drawn.

If a hunter has an application permit and an elk is outside of the counties that are open, he or she can take the animal. This is to try and keep the elk from spreading into areas they do not want them to be.

It does seem a shame that an animal as magnificent as the elk has disappeared from our state. It seems even more of a shame that a place cannot be found for them to roam the hills of Indiana once again.

Just think of how the sound of a bulging bull elk on a cold frosty morning would stir the blood of a hunter, or anyone else for that matter.

With the success of the reintroduction of elk in Kentucky it goes to show that it can be done. Other eastern states are also trying their luck at bringing elk back to where they once lived. Yes, it only takes some money, a little work, and a willingness to replace what we have lost and elk could once again call Indiana home.

Chapter 12

First published in the Boonville Standard on May 4, 1994.

Just leave it to a Beaver

One of the reasons our country was prosperous in the early days was because of the fur trade, and the most important furbearer at the time, was the beaver. The European beaver was already rare during America's pioneer days because they had been trapped out.

When the first explorers and trappers moved across North America, they discovered great numbers of beavers. Nearly every stream, creek and river contained them. Soon trading posts were set up in the wilderness, and in a short time, they were thriving communities.

During the taming of the American wilderness, not only were the great forest felled, but countless swamps and marshes were drained as well. Since beaver were the number one animal sought for its fur, it numbers steadily decreased. By the mid-1800's they were gone from most of their former range south of Canada.

The beaver disappeared from Indiana during the 1840's as they did from most Midwestern states. As late as the 1930's, they were confined mainly to the Rocky Mountains, the more remote parts of the Great Lakes States, and northern Maine.

People all over were concerned that the beaver might die out completely. Then in 1937, the Federal Aid in Wildlife Restoration Program started. During the first ten years, 27 states began research and restocking programs for the beaver. These states moved over 8,000 beavers into areas where they had long been absent; in some cases, for nearly a hundred years.

Beaver were brought to Indiana from Wisconsin and released into streams throughout the state. In a few short decades, they multiplied and moved into new areas. Then after more than 100 years, it was a common sight to see their familiar handy work.

The engineering work of the beaver is a marvel. They know just where and how to dam a stream to create a pond. Beaver ponds are very important for wildlife. Ducks and other water birds nest around their edges, and it cuts down on soil erosion. Long ago, the dead trees in their flooded lakes were the homes of woodpeckers and then purple martins.

When beavers cut trees from the banks of a stream to build their dam or to eat, it allows more sunlight in; this in turn causes more vegetation to grow. Many times, what grow are willow trees, and willow bark is one of the beaver's favorite foods. They will store large quantities of branches underwater in the autumn, so even if the water freezes over, their food source will still be available.

The beaver is the largest rodent in North America, reaching 40 to 60 pounds. There are even records of 90 to 100-pound beavers. Only the South American capybara is larger. Their fur is soft, well insulated, and water proof. This makes their fur very beautiful and valuable, and is still made into luxurious coats. Today, however, the season for taking beaver is regulated and not many people pursue them. Even though the pelts are very expensive after they are made into a coat, the trapper only receives a few dollars for each one.

Although the beaver is very interesting and an ingenious engineer, they can sometimes be a problem. Since they do not care what kind of tree they cut to build their dam, they can oftentimes cut valuable timber.

I once transplanted some bald cypress trees along Cypress Creek where I lived. I found several growing along a nearby swamp, and since they were close together and would eventually crowd each another, I knew by removing a couple it would allow the others to grow better. After digging up three from the gooey, sticky mud and carrying them about a half mile through the hot and humid, mosquito infested swamp, I arrived at their new home along the creek bank. After several backbreaking minutes, I planted the first. Then I had to repeat it all over again for the second and the third. Each time, I had to dig a new, deep hole in more sticky, gooey mud. Finally, however, the job was complete and they were now in the sun and should be happy there. I could also see them from my kitchen window. Almost all of the large cypress trees had been cut down when they built the dam near Newburgh and this swamp was the most northern place up the Ohio River in Indiana where wild bald cypress trees grew.

Soon the little trees began to grow and add beauty to the shoreline. That winter and for several winters after that, the floodwaters would rise, and then the water would freeze. After freezing, the water would fall and the sheets of ice would crush anything under them, including the trees I had so painstaking planted. The next spring, I would have to straighten the little cypress trees, sometimes putting a splint on the main shaft until it healed. After several years of taking care of the trees in this manner, they finally had grown large enough to withstand the weight of the ice sheets. Then one morning, I looked out the window and one of the trees no longer stood on the bank; a beaver had decided that it might be good to eat. After cutting it down, however, he decided he didn't like it after all and just left it lying there.

Sometimes they like to dam an area that causes water to flood roads, crops, standing timber or important real estate. They also enjoy gnawing on a variety of trees, sometimes picking an orchard; being a connoisseur of apple bark, you can see they can be very destructive.

Like most everything, there is good and bad. The beavers were here long before we arrived. They are just continuing their way of life, what they were designed to do. It is just that we are sometimes in their way. After all, the trees were made for the beavers, or were the beavers made for the trees? If you don't know the answer, just leave it to a beaver.

Chapter 13

Above is a River Otter caught by a local farmer in 2019. A very limited number are allowed to be trapped each season in Indiana.

Return of the River Otter

(This story was first published in my column in the Boonville Standard in 1993).

Most of the bird and animal species that we have lost in the Midwestern States were gone by the mid to late 1800s, but one held out until only one generation ago —— the river otter.

The last known otter in my state of Indiana was seen at Hovey Lake in the southwestern tip of the state in 1942. Then in the summer of 1986, an unconfirmed sighting took place near the Ohio River, in Warrick County, along Cypress Creek. Since this, a few other early sightings have been reported. According to a letter I received from Tom Edwards, Kentucky's south-central district wildlife biologist, there was a sighting in 1992 by an Indiana biologist. This otter was believed to have been one released in Grant County, Kentucky, in 1991.

This first unconfirmed sighting, since they disappeared from Indiana, happened to have been seen by me. I had walked out of the house to the backyard, which overlooked Cypress Creek. As I stood there, I noticed a fairly large brown animal swimming in the center of the creek towards the bank and me. Instantly I noticed that it didn't seem "normal." I had lived on the creek since I was fifteen years old and saw muskrats, beaver, mink, and even once, a groundhog swimming the creek, but this caught my attention because of its long body, which appeared to be about three feet in length. As my luck would have it, my two youngest children, Elijah and Jeremiah, who were but two and three, came out to see what I was doing. Turning towards them for just a second or two, animal had already gone from beneath the bank, where I couldn't see it, and was disappearing into the weeds about twenty feet from the creek. I mowed the grass all the way to the creek so it was an open area and this animal had traveled that gap in a matter of a couple of seconds. This also told me that it was not an animal I was used to seeing. I also saw that its rump was rather high as it went into the weeds, another sign that it was an otter. I knew all the other animals well that it could have been and being in the early afternoon most were not out. This was also an indication that it was an otter. It was the right size, length, shape and had the speed and habits of an otter.

I was so excited at what I saw that I left immediately to visit my parents, who lived just down the road, and to tell them what I just saw. As I was leaving, I told my oldest son Danny and his younger brother David and they went out and watched the creek where I told them I had seen it.

As soon as I left, the animal came out again and Danny got a good look at it. It came out of the weeds, ran to the edge of the creek, turned around, ran back in, then coming out a second time, turned and disappeared once more into the bushes. At the age of six, Danny could identify 80 species of birds and he knew animals very well too. By the time of this sighting, he was a teenager and knew many more. He said it was definitely a river otter. He said he got a good look at its large tapering tail and its head.

Later I contacted Scott Johnson, non-game wildlife biologist, from Indiana's Division of Fish and Wildlife and asked if Indiana had released any otters in the area. He told me that other Midwestern states were conducting river otter restoration projects and individual otters may occasionally wander into southwest Indiana by way of the Ohio and Wabash Rivers. Cypress Creek emptied into the Ohio only a mile away.

In a later correspondence, I asked if there were any plans to reintroduce river otters into Indiana. At the time, he said there weren't because their efforts and funds were being directed towards the peregrine falcon restoration project and there were no suitable habitats located as of yet.

This all changed a short time later and Mr. Johnson informed me that plans were being made to obtain 25 river otters from Louisiana for release in Indiana. This was a pilot program to see how well they would do. The release was successful and later between 1995 and 1999, a total of 300 otters were released and they soon began to multiply and spread. They are now in 63 counties.

In the summer of 2011, my neighbor, David, saw the first otter of his life and he saw it in Perry County where I now live. He's a trapper and hunter and each year traps dozens of beavers, muskrats, mink and even foxes and coyotes, but never saw an otter until this year.

This is another success story of bringing an animal back that had totally disappeared. Kentucky did not lose all their otters, but only a handful clung to existence until the tiny population was supplemented with ones brought in and released. This has also happened in other Midwestern states and there are already limited trapping seasons being implemented in some of them. It is just a matter of time before their population levels get high enough to do the same in Indiana.

With protection, the bobcat is increasing in Indiana and other states close by and even the cougar and black bear are showing up in places that they have been absent from for over a hundred and fifty years. I remember writing an article in my newspaper column in 1994 and predicting the return of the cougar and eventually the black bear to Indiana. Some laughed at me. Then in May, of 2010, a cougar was confirmed in our state. They have been seen more and more regularly in other states in the east, south and Midwest. So, has the black bear. In recent years, bears have moved into Kentucky, Ohio, and Illinois. If things continue and enough habitat is left, they will show up here too. There have already been reports of them.

In the Midwest, we lost and restored the white-tailed deer, the turkey, the beaver, the bald eagle and now the river otter. Now we can look forward to seeing something in its natural habitat that was gone. I am looking forward to once again having a viable population of otters in Indiana. It will feel good to get back something we have lost. It has been a long time since our streams have had the playful otter swimming in them. It also has been too long since an otter "slide" has been seen along their banks. Since the return of the river otter, it can be enjoyed by not only hunters and trappers, but also by all who venture into the wild.

This is the place on Cypress Creek where I saw the first river otter in Indiana since they disappeared in 1942.

Chapter 14

The White-tailed Deer

Above, I am standing with the first white-tailed deer I ever shot with a muzzleloader. The doe was taken with a CVA .45-caliber Kentucky rifle kit that I put together myself.

If I was not able to write this story, none of us would ever have had the opportunity to go after this big game animal. Most do not even know the history of the game animals they hunt. This story was first published in 1994. It was shortly after I did a wildlife news segment for the FOX 44 television station in Evansville, Indiana. Here is that story:

The last known, native white-tailed deer in Indiana was killed in Knox County in 1893 and for several decades, deer were absent from the state. Then, beginning in the

1930's, deer were brought in from Wisconsin, Michigan, Virginia and Pennsylvania to be released throughout Indiana.

Needless to say, the deer that were released in Indiana prospered and multiplied. By 1951, (the year I was born), the herd had grown to an estimated 5,000 animals. The first short hunting season was then opened for the first time since they had disappeared from the state. This first season consisted of a three-day season and only a few hundred animals (bucks only), were taken.

By the time I was old enough hunt in the mid-sixties, the annual harvest was around 5,000. It took several years of hunting with a bow and gun to take my first deer. Several deer have fallen since I took my first, and it seems hard to believe that only a few years ago, that many hunted all season without even firing a shot or seeing a deer.

This year (1994), it is predicted to be another record year with a total harvest of over 100,000 and the herd continues to grow.

Since the wolf and cougar are gone from Indiana as well as many other areas, man is the deer's number one predator, and he alone is responsible for the deer's wellbeing.

Deer have increased so dramatically in some places, that they have become a nuisance. In other areas where there is no hunting, they have over populated and become malnourished or even starved to death. There is nothing pretty at seeing a magnificent animal, such as the white-tailed deer, die a slow and painful death due to starvation or disease.

A special tax that is taken from the sale of sporting arms and ammunition, and from hunting license fees, has funded the recovery of the white-tailed deer. However, without the dedicated work of wildlife officials, the white-tailed could have gone the way of the buffalo. Now, once again, sportsmen, as well as the young and old, who will never hunt, can enjoy the beauty and grace of Indiana's largest wild animal, the white-tailed deer.

Chapter 15

Photo taken by the author in Spencer County, Indiana.

Nature's Surprises

The outdoors is full of surprises. Taking a leisurely walk, driving down a road or even glancing out a window at home, you are likely to see another world. All of us that love nature see beauty and wonder all the time, but occasionally we may witness the rare, the strange or even the bizarre things in the animal kingdom.

I have spent countless hours in the outdoors and many more hours just watching nature. In that time, I have been witness to some things that I've only heard of and a few I have never even heard mentioned.

The other day, my wife, Lilly, was in the kitchen when she said, "There's a squirrel out here." No surprise, we see squirrels every day at the bird feeders. Why would she even mention one being there? I thought. "Well," I said. Then she added, "It's eating a bird."

"A bird!" I said, rushing to the kitchen window. I had heard of squirrels eating eggs and baby birds, but had never seen it myself. Sure enough, as I looked out the window a gray squirrel was sitting holding a female purple finch as it dismembered it. I know squirrels are cousins of the rat and I've had rats kill my pigeons and even had one go under a mother duck and take her young, but never had I seen this behavior by a squirrel.

Squirrels can have other peculiar habits too. Years ago, I shot five fox squirrels in fifteen minutes without taking more than a few steps, as they seemed oblivious to the shotgun blasts. I wrote a Field and Stream editor who told me he too had a similar experience with a horde of migrating gray squirrels. I wrote about this in my book, *Barnestorming the Outdoors*.

Other odd things I have witnessed was an opossum carrying its bedding under its tail; a Carolina wren with a good-sized lizard it had killed and a baby fence lizard allowing me to reach down and pet it. I also had a mother flying squirrel rushing right up to my feet trying to rescue her young from a dead tree I had inadvertently knocked down.

I saw a comical situation once along a creek where a small bass had a large bullfrog by the hind leg. The fish would drag the frog under the water, then the frog would drag the fish back to the surface. I don't know how long this went on, as I got tired of watching. I also saw a similar struggle with a young wood duck and a painted turtle. The turtle had the duck by the leg trying to pull it under and the duck kept struggling back to the surface. I intervened because I knew the turtle would eventually win.

Sometimes we might see a rare albino bird or animal. I've seen a few white deer, squirrels and even a pure white blackbird. Several times, I've seen blackbirds and others with a few white feathers and once a golden sparrow. This bird gave me the inspiration to write the book *In Search of a Golden Sparrow*.

Once while in the spring woods hunting mushrooms, I happened to flush a female woodcock. As she flew, I watched her carefully because they are rumored to carry their young between their feet when fleeing danger. This has never been proven and I did not see it that day. I did, however, see only one young at the nest. It was left behind and was running around the forest floor with its featherless wings held up calling for its mother as she flew and flittered nearby. Carrying their young would not be an impossibility. The male jacana or lily-trotter, which is smaller than the female (as is the woodcock) not only incubates the eggs, but carries the young under his wings until they are old enough to walk on the lily pads.

While I'm talking about woodcocks, I did see something I've only seen once and have never read about. I had downed one while hunting and when I went to retrieve it, I found it still alive in a small thicket. As I approached, the woodcock began to fan out its tail as a tom turkey and display. I assumed this is a display against rival males, but I have never heard of it before.

Years later, I shot a quail that fell in some honeysuckle vines. The vines were so thick and tangled that my lab, Princess, could not even get in, so I made her stay back until I cleared all the vines away. Expecting to find the bird as I removed the vines, I cleared every one and even raked my boot across the leaves on the ground, but it had vanished. The dog kept insisting, however, that the quail was still there. Therefore, I gave her the command to fetch. Then to my complete surprise, she walked over and reaching down to the nearly bare ground, pulled the struggling bird from a depression under the leaf litter. I should have known to trust her as I once saw her dive under the water and retrieve a wounded teal.

Some things in nature happen all the time but we usually are not there to see them. Titmice love to line their nests with hair and I once saw them plucking fur from a sleeping raccoon.

I once found a raccoon on a gravel road trying to walk on its hind legs. I remember it looked bizarre, like something out of a horror movie. Evidently, it had been hit by a car and was so badly deformed that it could no longer walk on all fours.

I've been charged by groundhogs and even a rabid bat and muskrat but I have saved the most extraordinary event for last.

Long ago, we had some gray foxes coming to the house and eating cat food on the front porch. I saw them often and I wondered what one would do if I caught it. Therefore, after locking the chickens and pigeons in their house, I put a spring on the chicken coop door. Then tying a string to a stick, which held the door open, I ran it to a window in the house. I then put some scraps of meat on the ground leading to inside the pen. Then, just before dark, the fox showed up. After finding the trail of meat, he proceeded to eat as he walked right into the coop. Pulling the string, the door slammed shut behind the unsuspecting fox. Then as expected, the fox ran around the pen crashing into the wire trying to get out.

Rushing outside, I neared the pen expecting the fox to even try harder to get out, but to my surprise, he ran towards me, climbed the wire and sat on a limb I had put in the corner for my pigeons to perch on. I had heard of gray foxes climbing trees but had never seen it myself. This, however, was not the most surprising thing it did. Expecting the fox to go wild with fear as I approached, it instead sat there looking at me. "This is incredible," I thought. "Why doesn't it act afraid?" Then to my utter amazement, I took a piece of meat it had missed and putting it to the wire the fox took it from my hand! I saw what was happening, but I still could not believe it. Calling my wife outside so she could be witness to this extraordinary event, she too fed the wild fox from her hand. If someone would have told me of this I would not have believed it. It happened, I saw it and I still have a hard time believing it. So, when you're outdoors or even look outside, be ready for nature's surprises.

Above is a male evening grosbeak.

Backyard Bird Feeding Stations

Back in 1975, I began feeding birds in my backyard for the first time. I was 23-years-old at the time and I have been feeding birds ever since. Over the years, I have had over sixty species of birds come to my feeding stations. Besides the common ones, I have had some very rare and unusual ones. From: bald eagles, vultures, Louisiana water thrushes, Canada geese, wood ducks, evening grosbeaks and others.

During the 1990,'s I conducted wildlife a program at a Library in Newburgh and had nearly one-hundred people to attend. I have heard that the greatest sport in North America is not football or any other ball game, but is bird watching. More people participate in watching birds than any other sport. It is easy to see why. Birds are fascinating. They come in all colors, shapes and sizes. They also have very different habits in the way they search for food, raise their young, mate and behave.

My second book, *In Search of a Golden Sparrow,* was written because I discovered a common house sparrow that had a rare gene mutation. The sparrow was white with gold wing patches. It was not a real golden sparrow, but it didn't matter because the book was to be fiction. Then after I began the book and while I was trying to photograph the white sparrow, I found with it, one that was pure gold!

In 2009, I founded a nature club called the Golden Sparrow Nature society. We had monthly meeting in a classroom, at Forest Park High School, in Dubois County, Indiana. Often, we had special guests such as falconers, nationally known photographers and others. We also took field trips from time to time.

Shortly after starting the club, I put up a bird feeder outside the classroom so the kids could enjoy birds coming to eat. I also put up a list of birds I expected to show up. It was in town and about 100-yards from any forest, so I figured there would be about 16 different kinds come. That first year there were ecactly16 different kinds that came to the feeder! There were, however, a couple that showed up that I didn't really expect to, and a couple that I thought would, that didn't. Since that first year, there have been at least 23 species of birds, which have come to the feeder.

What do you need to get started? Not much. You can buy a low-cost feeder or even make one. Put it near a window where you can see and enjoy the birds that come. A southern window is best during the winter so they birds will be somewhat sheltered from the cold wind.

The best food to use is black sunflower seeds. Many different species will come for these. A mixture of corn and other seed is good for ground feeding birds.

Sunflower seeds will attract cardinals, titmice, chickadees, nuthatches, finches of all kinds, doves, woodpeckers and others.

The corn and mixed seeds attract sparrows of all kinds, finches, doves, grackles, other blackbirds, flickers, and several others.

If you live in the country, you can even attract birds of prey such as eagles, hawks and vultures with road kill.

If you want to enjoy watching the birds even more, get a field guild so you can identify the different kinds that come. Better yet, find someone that is knowledgeable and learn from them. Many in my club were able to see birds on our field trips that they had never seen.

Once you set up a feeding station, it will not be long before the birds find it. Once they do, it seems that they spread the word and soon many more will be coming for a free meal. Some species of birds (mostly ground feeders) will usually not come unless there is snow on the ground where they cannot find food. The worse the winter, the more birds there will be searching far and wide for food, which will find your feeder.

Suet feeders are good for several kinds of birds too, but woodpeckers benefit the most. I have had all species of woodpeckers in the part of my state of Indiana come to my feeders. The most difficult to attract is the huge pileated woodpecker.

One of the rarest and most sought-after specie to attract to a feeding stations is the evening grosbeak. I have only had them during two different winters in all the years of my bird feeding.

To me it is exciting to get up on a snowy morning, sit at the kitchen table with a hot cup of coffee and watch the beautiful birds just outside my window. The crimson red of the cardinals and bright blue of the blue jays against the white snow makes the winter wonderland even more beautiful.

If you put out feed during the summer, you will have some birds coming that are only here during the summer months. Indigo buntings, blue grosbeaks, rose-breasted grosbeaks are a few. In addition, you can put out oriole feeders that attract not only orioles but also hummingbirds. The hummingbird feeder attracts both, but only the hummingbirds can reach through the tiny hole to get the food.

Therefore, if you want to enjoy nature from the comfort of your home get into bird feeding.

Chapter 17

My son Elijah's first fish with little brother, Jeremiah, 1986.

Taking the Kids Fishing

Living along Little Pigeon Creek in southern Indiana as a child, gave me plenty of opportunity to fish. And going fishing with my father was one of my favorite things to do. I suppose only the excitement of waking up on Christmas morning could be compared to the excitement of going fishing.

Today many kids are glued to the TV, watching one program after another, playing video games, or even getting into trouble. I think a lot of parents are missing out on special moments that the children and they would remember for a lifetime.

When I was growing up, fishing was a very simple and relaxing activity. I remember waking up on a beautiful spring or summer morning, having breakfast (which usually consisted of milk gravy and homemade biscuits) and my father asking if I wanted to go fishing with him. I would run and get the shovel to help dig the worms, as my dad found an old tin can to put them in. We usually went behind my grandmother's house or next to her chicken house to dig for the "fishin' worms."

With each scoop of dirt turned over, my eyes would search the clods as my father broke them apart with the shovel. Sometimes there would be none; sometimes only one or two; but when he hit a "good spot" there would be several. As I picked the large red worms from the clods, my anticipation of the day's fishing would grow. When we had fifty or so worms we would be ready to head down to the creek.

Back in the fifties, most families lived a simpler life. There were no microwave ovens, home computers, video games or many of the things we take for granted now. We didn't have a TV set until I was seven, inside plumbing until I was nearly ten or a phone until I was eleven.

To go fishing was a simple matter also. To start, you usually went to "the thicket" and cut a small slender sapling for a "fishin' pole." A cork from a bottle was the bobber, and sometimes a small washer was used as a sinker. Very simple, but I caught a lot of fish.

It seems today people make things more complicated in every aspect of their lives. Now they need the latest reel, a hundred-dollar rod and a vast assortment of artificial lures before they want to go fishing. Oh, and I forgot, they also need a fifteen or twenty-thousand-dollar bass boat. I never had a store-bought cane pole until I was a teenager and I was twelve before I had a rod and reel (for fishing on the bottom for catfish) and I don't feel that I missed out on anything. When I went to the muddy banks of Little Pigeon

Creek with my willow pole and a can of worms I was happy. My father would dig steps down the bank so he could easily reach the water to put in the stringer of fish we caught and so I would have a place to sit while fishing.

The stringer was made when we caught the first fish. By tying two short green sticks to a piece of fishing line a stringer was created. Then after threading the shortest stick through the mouth and gills of the fish, it was placed in the water and the long stick was shoved into the bank.

However, before this, I would thread a wiggling worm onto my hook. Then tossing the line into the water, I would anchor the pole by sticking it into the muddy bank, sit back and wait for a bite.

As a small child, the creek looked wide and deep and I would sit on the second or third step from the water. Every time I got a bite, I would be filled with excitement. I loved fishing, but I remember I also was also a little afraid. I was afraid that I would catch a giant fish that would pull me in and under the muddy water and there I would be lost in the deep, dark depths of a murky grave. Because while fishing we would often hear a huge splash upstream where a giant fish had come to the surface. Then as we looked upstream, we would see large waves rippling across the creek where he had been. There were very large fish in the creek because it flowed directly into the mighty Ohio River. Catfish weighing over forty pounds had been caught and my father once saw an enormous alligator gar nearly ten feet long lying beside his boat. There were also huge snapping turtles in the creek and I could see in my mind a giant turtle on my line pulling me into the water. Therefore, when I got a bite I was glad my father was close by.

Once I did get a bit from a large fish and as I pulled it up, I was barely able to get it out of the water. The fish was lying on the bank at the edge of the water as my dad ran to get it. I remember as he was putting the fish on the stringer I stood there trembling from the excitement.

Why am I reminiscing about my early years as a child? Because sometimes when we get older, we forget how a child sees and feels things. How exciting things are when we first experience them. These memories I have as a child, keeps the excitement alive each time I pick up my pole to go fishing with my boys.

I like the solitude of fly-fishing by myself sometimes, but there is something special when you take your children along and they catch a fish. You can relive the excitement through your children.

As soon as it's warm enough in the spring, there is no better time to have fun with your kids. You don't have to spend a fortune to get started. Buy or cut a cane pole, get some string (I like the limp braided nylon) a bobber or cork, and some long shank, number 6 or 8 hooks. (You need a small hook so bluegill can get it in their mouth, and you need a long shank so you can get it back out). Then find a pond, lake, creek, river or stream and take your kids fishing. Remember to show the children how to handle hooks safely and be careful handling the fish, for their fins can cause considerable pain. Bring plenty of bait, a stringer and you may want to bring a camera to capture on film their first fish. And have fun, that's what it's all about.

Part Two:

Stories From:
Life Along Little Pigeon Creek.

The following stories are from my book *Life Along Little Pigeon Creek*. They are about birds, animals or that mention them, so I wanted to include them in this book.

Chapter 18

Picture by my son, David Barnes

The Great Yankeetown Easter Egg Hunt

It was the spring of 1961, and we had just lined up side by side facing the area where the eggs were hidden. I suppose hidden was not the right word for it, because the eggs could easily be seen, and they were everywhere. They were in bushes, beside clumps of grass, and many were lying in the open on the bare ground.

The area for this particular "hunt" was the southwest corner of the Yankeetown Elementary Schoolyard. Mrs. Lerch stood beside the small class of eighteen. It was the presents of this small silver-haired lady, which kept a lid on the mayhem that was soon to erupt.

By the time I was in the fourth grade, I felt that I was too old for such things as Easter egg hunts. It didn't look very dignified. Besides, there wasn't any challenge involved. It wasn't like frog hunting, where the frogs could jump in the water and escape. The eggs just sat there, and they were so brightly colored, that you couldn't miss them. Looking for Easter eggs didn't hold a candle to mushroom hunting. Now there was a sport I liked. Sneaking through the spring woods where the vivid, green leaves were unfolding from every branch, and mayapples, ferns, and wildflowers were covering the ground. Where you had to search for the almost invisible quarry, that hid in and under the thick carpet of leaves. And while you were stalking one of the rare and elusive mushrooms, you would sometimes encounter other interesting creatures, such as a box turtle or snake, which added excitement to the hunt. I hardly think you could compare the two.

"On your mark! Get set!" Mrs. Lerch said, as I began looking down the line of kids who were pawing the ground in anticipation of gathering the lifeless eggs that lay before them.

Kenny and Johnny were in position as they leaned into the wind, so they could get off to a faster start, and to cut down on wind resistance, and drag to gain greater speed.

Jimmy was leaning forward on his crutches, as the others were digging in, getting ready to lunge after the nearest egg.

Terry, the one who looked like a miniature George Burns, stood erect, if you could call his posture erect.

Mrs. Lerch, then taking one step back, adjusted her wire-rimmed glasses and spoke the magic word, "GO!"

What ensued next, I couldn't believe.

The children were dashing here and there, to and fro, over here, then over there, like an old hen's chicks looking for bugs.

Gordon, Billy, Johnny, and Kenny were racing one another among growls, snarls, and threatening looks, which were coming from Gene, an unusually shy and timid kid.

The usually prim and proper girls were grubbing through the bushes and weeds, screaming and yelling, as they clutched the eggs tightly in their claw-like hands. Even Jimmy was going at top speed on his crutches, using them to shield the eggs and to threaten any rival that got too close.

"Such a display of childish behavior," I thought. I had never seen Mary, Marylyn, Linda, Krystal, Wanda, Norma and Ann act this way. The boys, yes, but not the girls.

I stood for a moment watching the disgraceful sight. Then after several seconds had passed and the eggs were disappearing like June bugs in a chicken pen, I decided that since I had an empty basket in my hand, I might as well put a few eggs in it just for appearance sake.

Casually I walked over to where one was lying, paused for a second thinking how silly it was to be participating in this unsporting event and reached down to pick up the egg. Suddenly, some wild kid with hideous laughter dashed in, snatched the egg from under my fingertips, and fled.

Slowly rising up, I then spotted another egg and strolled over to it with manners and dignity like a human being. When I reached the spot, however, another egg-crazed kid, who was running stooped over, grabbed it and ran for another.

After half a dozen or so futile attempts of egg acquisition, I gave up.

All the eggs were gone by now anyway, except for one unfortunate specimen. This one sorry looking egg had been hidden under a rock, a rock that had been stepped on several times by the mad egg hunters while they were scampering and scurrying about searching for others of its kind.

This last egg had been discovered under the trampled rock, but it had been rejected and cast aside. There it lay alone, mashed, broken, and abandoned on the cold ground. It was a very pitiful looking egg, lying there with its shell broken and its yellow insides protruding through its battered form.

The excitement of the hunt had turned the usually well-mannered and dignified class into an ugly mob! I never would have believed it!

Looking around, I saw several kids with their baskets full of eggs and still looking for more. Some kids had just a few and a look of disappointment as their eyes searched the empty terrain.

Silently I stood observing the class while holding the empty basket in my hand. Finally, one kid who had only a couple of eggs, reluctantly walked over to where the crushed and mangled egg laid in silence, stood over it, then, reaching down, took it in his hands and gently placed it in his basket.

I didn't get any eggs that day, but the hunt taught me a lesson in human nature. A lesson of just how ugly a class can become when it is ruled by selfishness and greed!

After the "hunt" was over, I quietly followed the vociferous, jubilant mob, back into the classroom and took my seat. It was now time to award the kid who "found" the most eggs.

"Okay, class," instructed Mrs. Lerch. "I'll call your name and you tell me how many eggs you found."

Everyone was busy counting their eggs for the tenth time, just to make sure they hadn't over looked one.

"Johnny," Mrs. Lerch continued, "how may did you find?"

"Thirteen," he beamed.

I think it was he, who snatched the egg from under my fingertips, but I'm not sure, all I saw was a blur as he swept past me.

"Terry?" she asked again.

"Three," he answered with his ain't I cute and clever grin.

"Three?" I thought. "He shouldn't have counted that last egg. It was hardly recognizable after all it had been through." I suppose, however, if he started each morning with a shot of whisky and a cigar, he wouldn't be too choosy about his egg collection.

Mrs. Lerch continued down the row. "How many did you find Jimmy?"

"Nine," he replied.

"Six," said the next child.

"Eleven," answered another.

Then it was my turn.

"Kenneth, how many eggs did you find?"

I sat there for a moment, not wishing to answer, because I knew what the reaction of the class would be.

"None," I said, and immediately everyone turned in their seats and looked at me. They had a puzzled look, as if to say, "What happened? Why didn't you find any? What is wrong with you? What kind of excuse do you have?"

And I was thinking, "If you all hadn't put on a display of such appalling behavior and acted like greedy animals, I would have some eggs." I was also much too shy to explain that I felt I was too old for such things as Easter egg hunts. I didn't think they would understand.

"You didn't find any?" Mrs. Lerch asked in an unbelieving voice.

"No," I replied.

But all was not lost. I received a prize for finding the least number of eggs. I suppose Mrs. Lerch felt sorry that I was so unfortunate. And Ann shared some of her eggs and candy with me, which made me very happy.

Chapter 19

The Ingenious Trap

"You guys stay in the house! And don't come out!" I said. "I'm tryin' to catch a bird."

I was speaking to my two little brothers who did not understand the intricacies of the fine art of bird catching. I had just set a trap for the rare and elusive *passer domesticus,* better known as a house sparrow or English sparrow, commonly called spatcie, by country folks.

Daddy had built a birdhouse that spring and we had a pair of bluebirds building in it. Soon after they began building a nest, however, they were evicted, and driven away by a ruthless gang of house sparrows.

The birdhouse stood on a wooden pole, which sat just below the drive on the hillside. By standing in the drive, you could see into the holes where the spatcies had stuffed their nesting materials. Sticking out of the holes, were dead grass, pieces of twine, leaves, paper, sticks, and other assorted refuse.

For days, I watched the sparrows' feeding habits, their movements, and their daily routine, until I had a good idea of how to capture one alive. However, my plan had to be carried out with split-second timing. There was no room for error, because if things didn't go just right, my intended quarry could escape, or worse yet, may not survive.

I had noticed during my extensive research, that one of the birds always flew to the birdhouse from the woods across the road. It would come from the woods, fly across the road through the yard, then over the drive to its nest. It made the trip repeatedly throughout the day.

Sneaking (I mean borrowing) a chair from the kitchen and a morsel of bread, I placed the chair in the center of the drive. This was directly in the flight path that I figured the bird would take.

Very carefully, I then put the piece of bread in the trap and set it in the middle of the chair. I had to do this quickly. I had watched the birdhouse until I saw the intended victim (I mean bird) leave and fly across the road to the woods. I now had to get everything ready before it returned.

After the trap was all set, I hurried to the house and got behind the screen door on the front porch. Standing there, I began to feel the thrill of the hunt and the excitement of the chase. I kept looking across the road, straining my eyes to see the bird coming my way. Then after what seemed a long time, I spotted something near the woods. At first, it was but a tiny speck on the horizon over the woods. Closer and closer the little brown dot came and I was overtaken with apprehension as I peeked from behind the screen door.

Watching with nervous anticipation, the bird flew exactly where I thought it would. It came over the road, the drive, and then the chair. It was flying high and fast and I was wondering if it would see the tiny piece of bread in the trap below. My question was soon answered for the bird then did a sharp turn in the air, and dropped from the sky, spiraling down to land on the edge of the chair.

Now my bird was only inches away from the trap. But would it take the bait? Would the trap work? If it did, would the bird survive? I also would have to reach the bird quickly or it could escape.

Cautiously the bird hopped closer and stopped. Then hopping once more, it stood directly in front of the trap. I kept watching as it began craning its neck and looking the trap over carefully.

I had the trap facing the right direction. All calculations were perfect so far. But would the bird be fooled?

Finally, after what seemed like a long time, the bird lowered its head, leaned forward, and then——SNAP, he was caught!

Running as fast as I could, I reached the flopping bird and quickly released it from the mousetrap. At last, I had the wild bird in my hands, and it seemed completely unharmed, except for a few ruffled feathers.

After a minute or two of admiring my prized catch and pondering the ingenious way that I had captured it, I decided I better put it in a safe place. It was then that I discovered a flaw in my plans. I had failed to ready the cage for the expected guest. The old birdcage, which my parents had unwisely thrown away, but which was in perfect condition (except for the rust and a few bent places), was presently occupied. "No problem," I thought, "I'll just take out the box turtle and it will be ready for my bird."

Taking the cage and setting it on the ground, I knelt down beside it and began trying to get the turtle out. I soon found, however, that holding a struggling bird in one hand and trying to remove a turtle, which was wider than the door, was not very easy. After several minutes of futile effort, I determined that I would have to use both hands to extract the turtle.

About this time, my little brother Tom ran out to see what I was doing. In fact, it was hard to do anything without Thomas being present.

"What's the matter?" he asked, walking up and looking down at me struggling with the cage and turtle.

"I cain't get this stupid terrapin outta the cage," I answered with aggravation. "I need to use both hands, but I ain't got nowhere to put the bird."

"I'll hold him."

I looked up, trying to read his face, "You'll let him go."

"No, I won't," he insisted.

I was in a spot. Thomas was not one to be trusted, but I didn't have much choice. "Are you sure?" I asked, as I started to hand him the bird.

He nodded, "I'll hold him."

"Okay, hold him. Hold him real tight, and don't let go for nothing!"

Handing Thomas the bird, I cautioned him once more. "Make sure you hold him tight!"

"I will," he assured.

As soon as the bird was in his hands, I turned to the cage and began trying to get the turtle out. I hurriedly took hold of the turtle and worked it through the cage door. "There," I thought, "I got it!"

The second the turtle came through the door, however, I heard Thomas yell, "OUCH!" and looking up, I saw my bird flying away.

"Thomas! Why did you let my bird loose for?" I asked with sadness.

Thomas just stood looking at the disgust on my face, and then he timidly gave his excuse. "He bit me."

"He bit you? I said with aggravation. "He bit me too, but I didn't let him go!"

After giving him a threatening look, Thomas decided to go back in the house where it was a little safer. I sat down on the lawn, put the cage on my lap, and for several minutes stared through the open door at the empty cage.

Later, I tried again to catch another bird with the trap, but all attempts failed. They were just too smart to fall for the same trick twice.

Note: The house sparrow is a non-native species in America. It is considered a pest in most places in America and is not protected. It also was fair game for a little boy in the 1950's to try to catch as a pet.

Chapter 20

The Elusive Quarry

I did not give up, however, on trying to catch a wild bird. Soon after the escape of my prized catch, I heard the weak but audible chirps of baby birds coming from inside the birdhouse.

After waiting several long days, I figured that they were ready for capture. My plan this time was to be a straightforward one, with seemingly no problems.

Walking up to the birdhouse pole, I grasped it with both hands and began shaking and rocking the birdhouse back and forth.

It worked like a charm, for in just a minute or so, one unfortunate baby bird came tumbling out. Elated, I started for the little bird, but much to my dismay the baby bird wasn't the only thing that came out of the birdhouse. Almost immediately, a swarm of angry wasps were buzzing around everywhere. I could tell that they were upset and hostile by the way they were biting and stinging the birdhouse.

Sensing that they might be a threat to my well-being, I made a hasty and swift retreat towards the safety of the front door of the house. At the same time, one of the more intelligent members of the wasp swarm saw me fleeing the scene and figured that I was the one responsible for all the commotion. He also figured that I should be taught a lesson.

By putting on a burst of speed, the wasp soon overtook me. Landing on the back of my hand, I watched him sit there and take out his anger by making the point that I should never bother him or his kind ever again. It did not work, however, because ever since that day, wasps and I have been bitter enemies.

After the wasps calmed down somewhat, I dashed in and retrieved my baby sparrow. Even though I had to go through some pain to finally get a little bird, I felt it was all worth it, even if it was just a spatcie.

I put my little bird in the old birdcage, made a perch for him from an old stick I found in the yard, and sat down to admire my new pet.

Over the next few days, I would take him out often and hold him. He was cute, as he would sit on my finger chirping and opening his wide, yellow mouth to be fed.

About this point in time (and long afterwards), my little brother Thomas began having a great curiosity about how things were made and how they worked. Often by using the "tools of his trade" (usually a hammer), he would take my toys apart, to discover, examine, and study their intricate internal mechanical design.

One day soon after the capture of my baby bird, I was outside playing, when Bill came out of the house and walked up to me. He looked a little concerned as he neared so I turned to him to see what he wanted. "Kenny," he said, and I could tell by the sound of his voice that it was bad news. "Tom just killed your baby bird."

"Thomas did what?" I asked sadly. "How did he do that?"

I thought that perhaps he had been playing with it and somehow accidently dropped it or stepped on it or something. Bill then explained how Thomas wanted to discover, examine, and study the bird's intricate internal mechanical design by disassembling it.

Chapter 21

Tater Patch Pet

After my dad had planted the garden that spring, he spaded up a small spot for me. It was tiny, only about six feet wide and eight feet long. In it, I had a few vegetables, but over half was planted in potatoes. Nearly every day I would come and check my garden to see how it was doing.

On one particular day, I was walking through my garden looking at my potato plants. Stopping, I stood there admiring how big they had grown. As I was looking down, I happened to notice something that seemed odd under one of them. It was almost totally hidden by a large, potato leaf. As I looked closer, however, I could make out two, small, buggy eyes, and I saw that it had dark fur.

"It looks like a baby animal," I thought, but I was a little apprehensive about reaching down and picking it up not knowing for sure what kind of creature it was. "It's not a mole," I was thinking, "and it doesn't look like a rat." I kept standing there trying to figure out what it was. I had to make a decision fast, however. If it was a baby animal I did not want to run the risk of losing it for a pet, so I decided to take the chance.

Very carefully, I began reaching down, keeping my hand behind it and obscured by the potato plants. Then when my hand was very close, I made a quick grab, and——I had it!

Lifting it from under the foliage, I saw what it was——it was a baby rabbit!

"Boy, oh boy!" I said aloud. "I've got a baby rabbit!"

Quickly I ran up the hill to the house to show everyone what I had caught.

The old birdcage came in handy once again. Putting some dead grass in it for bedding and some water, I ran back down to the garden and snatched some fresh lettuce. The tiny bunny was so small that the birdcage made a roomy home.

I stood watching my new pet for a long time, but he just sat there with the lettuce in front of him, and he seemed to have no interest in eating it.

"I have to get him to eat," I thought, "or I won't be able to keep him."

Taking him from the cage, I sat down and held him in one hand on my lap. Then taking a piece of the lettuce from the cage with my other hand, I put it to his mouth, but he just sat there, refusing to even take a nibble.

Undeterred, I then took a stiff part of the lettuce leaf and pushed it in the little bunny's mouth. He just sat there staring, however. Pushing the lettuce in a little farther, he bit down——then he munched——then he began eating. After that, he would eat all that I would give him. He even ate out of my hand and I knew that my baby rabbit would live.

It was no time that he outgrew the old birdcage. After a brief search, I came up with an orange crate for his new home. Taking him and the crate outside, I put him inside of it. The crate was very roomy compared to the little birdcage and the little rabbit seemed to be very content.

I kept a brick on the lid to keep him from getting out and every morning I would go outside to feed and admire him.

Then, early one morning, a few weeks later, when I went to feed him, I saw that the brick was not on the lid. In fact, I did not see the brick anywhere.

Walking closer to the crate, I kept trying to see any sign of him through the slates, but I saw nothing. Reaching

for the lid, I was still hoping that he would be inside. He had
grown so much, that by now, he was nearly half grown, and
I looked forward to feeding him every day and watching
him eat. Slowly I raised the lid and looked inside. My heart
sank, for my little rabbit was gone. "Thomas! Thomas did
it," I thought. "He must have taken the brick off and let my
rabbit escape."

Thomas denied it of course, and I never could prove
that he was the one that let my rabbit loose, but it didn't
matter, my tater patch pet was gone.

Chapter 22

Day of the Groundhog

East of our house, down the gravel road about half a mile, lived Eugene, my grandpa Finley's son. Here I would often visit Eugene, his wife Ellen, (my second cousin) and their three children.

Betty was the oldest, about three years older than I was. Amos was one year and two days younger than I was, and Jackie, his little brother, was about three years younger than he was. A few years later, there would be another girl named, Carolyn.

Next door to Eugene, and on the same property, was my mother's Uncle Franky.

Franky was a tall thin man and very laid back. He enjoyed playing the fiddle. I also remember that he had an old mule that he used to plow his garden every spring. The mule looked old even when I was a child and lived long after Great Uncle Franky died.

I always liked visiting their house because Amos and Jackie usually had some kind of animal for a pet, too. Once they had a raccoon. Sometimes they'd have baby turtles or a collection of toads, "hoppy toads" as Jackie called them. The strangest animal they ever had, however, were none of these. Once they dug a baby groundhog out of its den and made a pet out of it.

When young, the groundhog often played with them as a kitten would. It stayed in the house, in a box, where it would come and go as it pleased.

When it became full-grown it went in and out of the house just like a cat or dog, and every morning would come inside for breakfast. Sometimes while Ellen was cooking at the stove, it would walk up and begin very gently nibbling on the calf of her leg to get her attention.

The groundhog ran lose all over the yard and woods, but always stayed near the house. The woodchuck was a female and the following spring she made a den in a bank just across the gravel road. One day, soon afterwards, the groundhog was on her way back to the house. While trying to cross the road, however, a woman was speeding down the road in a car and ran over her.

Later on, the boys caught another little groundhog. This time, it was a male. He played when he was young like the little female had, but when he grew older he wasn't as gentle as the one before. Every time I visited Amos when he had this pet, I would stay in the car until Amos told me of its whereabouts. This was because of what happened on a previous visit.

My Uncle Emmett and I had come together for a visit. Coming in the yard, we saw no one around. We then proceeded to the kitchen door to knock. I stood behind Emmett as he knocked on the door. While we were standing there waiting, I thought I saw something move under the floor of the house near Emmett's feet. The house was small and very old and was built only a few inches off the ground.

Suddenly I saw the groundhog's head as he lunged forward, grabbing Emmett's boot with his sharp rodent teeth. The groundhog then began growling and trying to drag the boot, with Emmett's foot inside, under the floor.

"What in the world!" Emmett exclaimed as he jumped back trying to shake the groundhog loose.

The woodchuck, however, was hanging on, still growling and still trying to pull Emmett's foot under the floor.

Finally, Emmett broke free and we hurriedly dashed into the safety of the house, and we were both greatly relieved when the door shut behind us.

Chapter 23

A Legend Comes Alive

Along Little Pigeon Creek in the 1950's there was a legend. It was a legend of a man, a man who roamed its muddy banks and wandered the nearby forest. Summer and winter, he went barefoot, wearing only a pair of black trunks and a huge knife that hung from his side.

He often swam the creek and swung across it on long grapevines that were suspended from the tops of tall, overhanging trees. He walked with long strides that made it impossible to keep up with him, unless you ran. In winter, he broke ice to swim and hunted game with only his knife. The knife, he made himself, from a leaf spring of an automobile. He used his knife so often that it was like a part of him. He was not, however, just a legend, although few outside the area knew of, or believed in him. This legend was real and alive, and he was called——Tarzan!

An Evansville newspaper once captured him on film. They called him "Yankeetown's Tarzan." He was photographed in the center of town in front of Ada Graham's store. Tarzan was squatting in the snow wearing his usual "attire" next to Ada, who was wearing a fur coat.

There's a story of someone from outside the area that once had a near close encounter with the legend. The man happened to be fishing under a bridge that spanned Little Pigeon Creek close to Yankeetown. Suddenly, upon hearing a blood-curdling yell coming from downstream, the man looked to see a nearly naked figure swing out over the creek on a grapevine and drop into the water. The figure swam to shore, climbed the muddy bank, and then strode down the creek.

Quickly the shocked and frightened man began gathering in his lines, then made a hasty retreat; presumably, to find a quieter place and one that was a little more civilized.

Tarzan stood about five-foot ten inches tall, had dark hair, and was slender, but very muscular. I was told that he had a tree house in the woods on the small farm where he lived, but I was too young to visit him to see it. When I first remember him, he was about forty years old and I was about five or six. He was a man of few words, but for a little boy, he was a man that made life an adventure, and full of excitement.

"Here comes, Tarzan!" my little brother, Bill, yelled.

Looking up, I saw him walking into the drive.
Quickly I left my toys on the ground that I had been playing
with and ran out to meet him.

He was nearing the house when ran up and stopped in
front of him.

"How are you doing?" Tarzan asked, as I stood in the
drive awe struck, that the local celebrity had come for
another visit.

"Okay," I replied, staring at the giant knife that was
hanging from his waist.

I always liked it when Tarzan visited; not too many
kids have a real Tarzan that lives close by.

"Can I see your muscle, Tarzan?" I asked.

Tarzan looked down at me to watch my reaction as he
stretched out his arm, then drew it up, flexing his muscle.

I stood there awed by the size of his biceps. At the
time, I didn't know the name of the muscle; to me it was just
"the muscle."

"Let me see yours," Tarzan requested.

Proudly I put up my arm to show him my bicep.

"Boy, that's a big one," he said, and it was. I got it
from climbing trees all the time.

Tarzan was a big influence on me, and I was always
trying to obtain great strength.

"Can you do this?" Tarzan asked, reaching down with
his toes and picking up a fair-sized brown stone from the
drive. Clutching the rock between his big toe and the next
one, he took aim at a nearby tree. Drawing back his leg, he
let the rock fly. Sailing through the air and with a
resounding crack, it struck the tree.

I then picked up a rock between my toes and tossed it
toward the tree. It did get there, but barely, and missed the
tree by two or three feet. I did not think that I did that bad,
after all, Tarzan had been practicing a lot longer than I had.

After talking with me a while, he started down the
path to my grandmother's house with me following close

behind. I struggled trying to walk to keep up with him, for I knew what he often did there.

Walking just behind him, we came to the house, and then went around to the front yard and stopped. I stood there watching, as he then walked over to a large tulip popular tree next to the holler that was about thirty feet away from where I was standing. After reaching the tree, he turned and began walking back towards me, pacing off several steps. Nearing me, he stopped and turned to face the tree. I now knew he was going to do what I loved seeing him do the most.

My eyes were glued to the long, black, leather sheath hanging from his waist, then he reached down, and slowly pulled out the giant knife. It was nearly a foot and a half long, with brown leather bound around its handle. It was a very impressive looking weapon. Intently, I watched as he held the knife above his head by its pointed end. Then extending his arm and the knife out in front of him, he took careful aim at the tree.

A large wound was on the side of the tree, where he had thrown his knife so many times before, and now the wound became his target.

Slowly Tarzan raised the knife up behind his head and anxiously I stood beside him watching. A look of determination suddenly came on his face as he drew back the knife even farther. Then in one swift motion, he leaned forward and flinging his arm, let the knife go sailing through the air. It flew end over end as it rushed towards its mark. Then with great force, it stuck deep into the center of the wound on the side of the tree.

After several minutes of practicing throwing his knife, he returned it back to its sheath, much to my disappointment.

"I've got to be going," he said, looking down at me and turning to walk away.

I stood there watching as he walked through the yard and up to the gravel road. Turning slightly and glancing back, he waved good-bye.

"Good-bye, Tarzan," I yelled, and standing there in Grammaw's front yard, I watched him walking down the dusty road until he was out of sight, on his way to visit more of his neighbors.

Chapter 24

The Panther

According to the book, *Alien Animals*, by Janet and Colin Bord, there were numerous sightings of large cats in the Midwest during the late 1950's. And on page 71 of their book, it tells of several sightings close to Little Pigeon Creek that were reported to the Warrick County Sheriff, who lived in Paradise, a town just a few miles west of our house.

On February 2, 1958, an Evansville newspaper had an article called *"Panther Eludes Army."* It tells of Sheriff Bob Shelton, leading three to four hundred armed men, trying to find it.

Back in "the hills", as we called them, there were many such stories about strange animals. Long before the newspaper article, there were rumors of big cats, and my grandmother often told me of this mysterious beast she called *the panther*. This rare and elusive beast was supposed to roam the woods along Pigeon Creek. She said it was very sly and came out only after dark to stalk the woods, looking for something or someone to fill its voracious appetite. I was also told that it was very intelligent and would often trick its intended victims by screaming like a woman in distress; then it would cry like a baby. When a person would come to help the woman, the panther would spring from its hiding place and pounce on the unfortunate victim with razor sharp claws and flashing saber-like teeth.

There were many that said they had heard its screams, and some had claimed to have even seen it.

One story is that a neighbor, Pat, was out one night hunting with his hounds, when all of a sudden, the dogs picked up the scent of "something". After a short time, Pat heard the dogs barking excitedly. They had "something" treed.

Arriving to where the dogs were, Pat saw a huge cat sitting on the ground with the baying hounds all around it. One dog was dead, and a couple of others were badly wounded. The man was so frightened that he left the dogs and ran home.

Several years earlier, a group of people in Spencer County claimed to have seen a very large brown cat with a long tail, run across an open field.

Whether the panther existed or not, did not matter, because I believed it did. When you're that young, you will believe almost anything anyone tells you, because you haven't learned anything yet. I didn't even know what was across the creek. I knew there was a big forest, but I didn't know how big, or what kind of animals could live there. A small child's mind cannot comprehend too much. I also figured that adults knew a lot more than I did about such things; after all, they had been around forever.

I once nearly met the legendary creature on the banks of Little Pigeon Creek. It was an experience that I shall never forget.

When I was seven years old, my dad and a friend of his were going to run their fishing lines late one evening, and as they were going to the creek, I followed.

Standing on the bank, I watched as they got in the small, wooden boat and started paddling down the creek. As I watched them going farther and farther downstream, I noticed it was beginning to get a little dark. Standing there, I was thinking that at any moment, they would stop and start coming back, but they kept going further and further down the creek and it kept getting darker and darker. Then they disappeared around the bend of the creek and were out of sight. Now, I stood on the lonely creek bank all by myself, in the dark woods, with the panther stalking somewhere nearby! "He may be lying along the path on the way back to the house!" I thought. "Should I stay and wait for my dad to return, or should I try and make it back home alone before the panther comes out?"

It was getting darker by the minute, and the path leading home was very narrow with weeds and bushes leaning into it, making it even more dark and shadowy. All these thoughts raced through my mind. My decision had to be made quickly. "The panther could be coming down the creek even now!"

I began to hear night sounds of insects, frogs, and an owl close by as I glanced down the creek one more time to see if my dad was coming back yet, but he was nowhere in sight. "I better try and get home before it gets too dark to see the path," I thought, as I turned to go.

I had always thought of the panther as being coal-black and the darker it got, the harder it would be to see him. I didn't want to run up the path, because he might be lying in it, so I walked very slowly. Each step I took seemed to take forever, and I could feel and hear my pulse pounding in my ears. The woods began to come alive, with katydids calling, and a giant bullfrog bellowing nearby. Then I heard other noises. "It could be the panther!" I thought. "Don't look back, it may be following you! Don't run, you might run into the...!" I didn't want to think about it, but I couldn't help it. I was in its home, and it prowled the creek after dark. "Oh, I'll never come to the creek again, when it's so close to dark!"

Going up the path, I could feel the weeds and bushes brushing against my legs, like claws trying to pull me into them. Finally, after what seemed an eternity, I came out of the dark woods. Then running as fast as I could, I ran up the hill, past Uly's place, past the garden, and to the house. As I burst through the door, I was never so relieved to see light again.

Part Three:

Animals I have Raised or Cared For

The next section is about the birds and animals I have raised as babies or others which came to visit us. The raccoons, Buddy and Rambo have a book written about them and I have received a five-star rating and a great review of the book. The two orphaned raccoons were on the national television program Real Tv back in December of 1998. There are also several videos of them playing together and with my family on YouTube and GodTube, which are free to watch.

Chapter 25

Buddy is on bottom, Rambo on top.

Buddy and Rambo:
The Orphaned Raccoons

Above are Buddy and Rambo (Buddy is on bottom and Rambo on top). They were two, tiny baby raccoons that lost their mother. They were all alone and helpless. Then they were found and adopted by my family and me. I raised them to be released back into the wild. They never were caged, but were free to come and go as they pleased. I had to teach them how to find their own food in the wild and how to stay away from danger. I also tried to teach them to stay away from things they shouldn't bother, like chickens, bird feeders, and things growing in the garden, but with limited success.

Later, when they were a little older, I took some home video of them playing and getting into mischief. Soon they were TV stars and millions of people saw them on a national television show that was aired December 7th 1998. They now have several videos on YouTube and GodTube.

Chapter 26

Rufus the Fox Squirrel

I found Rufus on a path in the woods where he had crawled searching for his mother. Evidently, she had been killed by a hawk or other predator. He was so tiny that I had to feed him using a doll bottle. Here he is after he grew up. He is eating a small piece of bread and sitting in my backyard. I was standing only a few feet away when I took the photo. I have his story in some of my children's books.

Chapter 27

Taco the Softshell Turtle

Several years ago, my youngest son, Jeremiah, found this spiny softshell turtle. He was discovered in a small stream that was drying up behind our house. We named him Taco and put him in a goldfish bowl during one winter. The following spring, we put him back where we found in in the same stream, which then had water. Taco's story is also in some of my children's books.

Chapter 28

Groundhog's Day

This baby woodchuck, also called a groundhog, was found by my son, Jeremiah. The little guy was apparently ill. We cared for him for several days but he did not make it. He would have died even sooner if he had not been found. It is nature's way to weed out the weak but it is sad.

Chapter 29

A Full Bowl

Above are several baby turtles I had when I lived on Cypress Creek many years ago. From left to right are: a red-ear painted shell, a spiny softshell, a midland painted shell, another red-ear painted shell, another midland painted shell and at the bottom, is a common snapping turtle. I kept them all summer in the bowl but released them back into the creek in the autumn, so they could hibernate over the winter.

Above photo is of the same turtles sunning themselves.

Chapter 30

The Very Odd: The Opossum

Above is a young opossum I caught in the backyard. I just wanted his picture and released him after I took this one. I have raised baby opossums before but I do not have any photos of the ones I had as it was many years ago. Opossums are the only marsupial in North America. The female's pouch faces backwards and she carries her babies on her back once they are old enough to crawl from her pouch. If one falls off, they will be left behind. When they are born, they are no bigger than a honey bee with only front legs as their back ones are not formed yet. They then must crawl all the way to the pouch and attach themselves to a nipple to eat. If there are too many or if they can't make it to the pouch, they will die. They also have a prehensile tail so they can hold onto things.

Chapter 31

The Beasts of the Wild

Below are some of the wild creatures that have come to our cabin. I have written another book about my life and following my dream to be a writer. It is titled *A Cabin in the Woods*.

A baby fence lizard on our front porch. Beside it is the head of a 16-penny nail. The photo is about life-size!

This is a very old female Box Turtle. She has just about lost all the markings on her shell. She has looked this way for at least the last twenty-two years because that is when I first saw her. I would guess she is around seventy to eighty years old and maybe much older. She has been coming to the house each year for watermelon and cantaloupe, which we feed her. Here she is dining on a piece of beef sausage and strawberry tops.

Stubby was a wild raccoon, with a bobbed tail, that came to our front door each night wanting food. She became tame enough to take cookies from our hand. Here she is eating cat food on the front porch as I stand beside her taking the photo.

Above is a mother raccoon and her young that are coming to the house for something to eat. The young ones would take food from our hand. I do not advise anyone to do this unless you are very familiar with the animals and know that they can become dependent on handouts. We only did this a few times and stopped.

"You will have a covenant with the stones of the field and the wild animals will be at peace with you," Job 5:23.

Epilogue

I hope you have enjoyed reading this book. One of the most popular presidents in the United States was Theodore Roosevelt. He was an outdoorsman, a fisherman, and a sportsman that hunted all over the world. He was also a conservationist and is responsible in a great part for making Americans aware of the natural heritage we have.

If we conserve what we have and make room for the fellow creatures that call this planet home, there will always be room for all of us. We do not have the right to destroy what God has created. If He didn't want it, He wouldn't have created it. Everything has its place.

Today, humans are not only killing wildlife by illegal poaching, poisoning the air and water, but worse, they are destroying more and more habitat that wildlife needs to survive. Over the last two hundred years marshland, beaches, swamps, prairies, rainforests, deciduous forests and crop lands have been filled in, cut down, burned and bulldozed. Then the land that once supported a host of birds and animals has been used for factories, homes, landfills, or just obliterated for no other reason than they were there. These places were and are the homes of countless species of wildlife. Many of these species are rare, declining or have already been wiped off the face of the earth. My question is: How much longer will it be before there is no more room for our species? There *will* be a tipping point reached someday and it will be in the not too distant future. When this happens, our species will be in decline and will go extinct and very quickly, as did the passenger pigeon! The sad thing is, we are doing it to ourselves now.

I write about many biblical prophecies that tell us what the future holds and it is not pretty. The Bible agrees with what scientists say and common sense tells us: We can't go on destroying our world without dire consequences. We are already reaping what our forefathers and the previous generations have done. We have lost many unique and beautiful birds and animals from our planet. Those of the past had no concern that what they destroyed would not be for future generations to see and enjoy. I have listed a few of the birds and animals that we have lost but there are many more and as direct result of greed, selfishness and ignorance.

There are so many birds and animals that I can never see in the wild, at a zoo, or even on film that are gone forever. I'm getting old now and my days on earth are numbered. Those coming after me, however, will also miss out on having these birds and animals that have forever disappeared because of man.

We have lost some of the greatest creatures that have ever walked on earth. We lost the largest bird to ever live, the elephant bird that weighed 1,000 pounds! Also, the tallest bird, the giant moa that was nine feet tall and weighed 600 pounds. The Tasmanian tiger, or the Tasmanian wolf as some know it, is gone. It was the largest, carnivorous marsupial in Tasmania.

There are too many to list and we are losing more all the time. It often takes so little to save a species but nothing can bring them back. We have lost many birds and animals in my state of Indiana. Some I have listed. Some such as the prairie chicken was here in Indiana until very recently, but nothing was done to save it and now it is gone.

Many in America point their finger at others around the world for destroying the rainforest or killing all the birds and animals. We look back at the generations before us and blame them for destroying the buffalo, the great auk, the passenger pigeon, the Labrador duck, sea otter, Steller's sea cow and the dodo bird, just to name a few. Yet, we in America destroy cropland, build shopping malls and subdivisions on land that once supported a great diversity of wildlife. Surplus animals that are culled through limited hunting or fishing will recover and they will *never* die out. Once their habitat is destroyed, however, they have no home, no place to live and can never multiply again. Once they are gone, no matter how much habitat is restored they will not be there to replenish themselves. We were given this earth to be good stewards of it, not to destroy it. We are already reaping what we and others have sown. In the end, everyone will pay for what they have done to our precious, one-of-a-kind world.

Recently I wrote a book titled, *Thou Shall Not Kill: What Does God think about the killing of animals?* "There is a time and season for everything under the sun." One part of that scripture says, "There's a time to kill, and a time to heal…" Ecclesiastes 3:1-8. Today we need to heal the damage we've done to the earth and to many of the birds and animals in which we share the earth. In times past, we had to tame the wilderness. Now we must let the wilderness be free. We have won. We have not only subdued the earth, we have made it cry out for help.

There was a time that mankind was afraid of many of the wild creatures that roamed the earth and in days gone by, many people were killed by the beasts of the earth. Today, they are afraid of us, and rightly so. Now we can destroy any dangerous creature that dares threaten us with just the pull of a trigger.

We were created in the "image of God" and He gave us the earth and put us over all the creatures on it. Not to destroy, but to care for. We, like God, have the power and should have the wisdom to see into the future. We should be able to look behind us and realize the mistakes we have made and learn from them. If not, we are bound to repeat them all over again. We are doing that today and there will be a day of reckoning.

Here is one last thought and it is from the *one* that created everything. "The nations were angry *that* your wrath is come, and the time of the dead, that they should be judged, and that you should give reward unto your servants the prophets, and to the saints, and *to* them that fear your name, small and great; and *that you* **should destroy them which destroy the earth**," Revelation 11:18.

About the Author

Kenneth Edward Barnes has been called, *"A modern day Mark Twain"* by a local newspaper reporter. *"He shows a Twain sense of humor in conversation and in his writing. He writes in the 'down to earth' style that Twain used to capture the heart of America."*

He was born on April 4, 1951, along the banks of Little Pigeon Creek in the southern tip of Indiana, downstream from where Abraham Lincoln grew up. As a child, he loved fishing from the muddy banks of the creek and roaming in the nearby woods. He never missed an opportunity to be in the outdoors where he could see all of God's creation.

Ken is a nationally published writer, poet and the author of over one hundred books. Some of his most popular ones are: *The Mammoth Slayers; A Cabin in the Woods;*

Mysteries of the Bible; Madam President; Life Along Little Pigeon Creek; A Children's Story Collection; The Golden Sparrow; Buddy and Rambo: The Orphaned Raccoons; Outdoor Adventures; The Arkansas River Monster collection, and Do Pets go to Heaven? This could soon change, however, as he has recently written several others.

The author became a member of *Hoosier Outdoor Writers* in 1993, where he has won several awards from them in their annual writing contest. He has also been a guest speaker for the *Boy Scouts, Daughters of the American Revolution, Teachers Reading Counsel, Kiwanis Club*, and at several schools, libraries and churches.

Ken has been an outdoor columnist and contributing editor for several newspapers and magazines: *Ohio Valley Sportsman, Kentucky Woods and Waters, Southern Indiana Outdoors, Fur-Fish-Game, Wild Outdoor World, Mid-West Outdoors,* and a hard cover book titled *From the Field.* He has written for the *Boonville Standard, Perry County News, Newburgh Register and Chandler Post.* He has had poems published locally and nationally. One titled *The Stranger* went to missionaries around the world. The poem, *Princess,* was also published locally and nationally, and won honorable mention in a national contest. His best-loved poem is *Condemned* and has been published by the tens of thousands. Nearly every single poem he has written is in his colored paperback book, *Poems from the Heart* and *My Favorite Poems.*

Ken has worked for an Evansville, Indiana, television station where he had outdoor news segments aired that he wrote, directed and edited. He also had film clips that were aired on the national television shows *Real TV* and *Animal Planet.* At this time, he has several short videos on YouTube and on GodTube.

Studying nature since childhood, he is a self-taught ornithologist and a conservationist. In 2009, he became founder and president of the *Golden Sparrow Nature Society*, the name of which was chosen because of his first published book. Ken loves to share his knowledge and love of nature, and it has been said that he is a walking encyclopedia on birds and animals. Because of this, he recently published an e-book titled *Birds and Animals of Southern Indiana*. It has over 300 photos of birds and animals, most of which he photographed himself. He frequently updates it with new photos.

He has followed his dream of being a writer since 1978 and now lives in a cabin in the woods. Being an individualist, he cleared the land, dug a well by hand and built the house himself, which uses only solar electric. He even wrote a book titled *Solar Electric: How does that work?*

Reviews of the author's books can be seen or left on his **Author Page** at **Amazon Books**. All his books are listed on his author page under the name of Kenneth Edward Barnes. You can also find him on his **Facebook** page at: **Kenneth Edward Barnes** or on **Twitter** at **Kenneth Edward Barne @BarneKenneth.**

Books by Kenneth Edward Barnes in:
Paperback, Hardcover and E-book

1. In Search of a Golden Sparrow
2. Life on Pigeon Creek
3. Barnestorming the Outdoors
4. Invasion of the Dregs
5. A Children's Story Collection
6. Poems from the Heart
7. The B.O.O.K. (Bible Of Observational Knowledge)
Under the pen name of ZTW

Books available as E-books only:

1. Is There a Devil? Is Satan Real?
2. The Thirteenth Disciple
3. The Two Witnesses
4. The Mammoth Slayers: Why the series was written
5. Birds and Animals of Southern Indiana
6. The Ancient Art of Falconry
7. Solar Electric: How does that work?
8. The Book of WISDOM (Words Instructing Spiritual Direction Of Man)

9. Instruction Manual for the WIFE (Wonderful Idea From Eden)
10. How to Care for your MAN (Mate's Animalistic Needs)
11. How to Raise your CHILD (Cute Huggable Innocent Little Darling)
12. INSTINCTS (Interesting Nature Secret Tendencies If Nature Could Teach Secrets)
13. The Adventures of Ralph and Fred
14. Twelve Tantalizing Tongue Twisting Tales
15. The Last Mammoth
16. A Squirrel Named Rufus
17. Pete: The Poor Pig
18. The Bike Ride
19. The Great Yankeetown Easter Egg Hunt
20. King and Tippy: Two Special Puppies
21. The Wanderer of Little Pigeon Creek
22. The Panther
23. A Legend Comes Alive
24. The Eagle and the Hummingbird
25. The Grumbling Grasshopper
26. Buzz: The Cowfly
27. The Watermelon Turtle
28. I Don't want to be a Pig!
29. Who? What? When? Where? Why?
30. Buggies: (Also, includes: Animal Cracks and other jokes and riddles)

Available as Paperback and E-books:

1. A Biblical Mystery: Christians need to become a Jew: What does this mean?
2. A Cabin in the Woods
3. A Day Appointed
4. A House Divided: This is why Donald Trump won the election
5. A Rude Awakening
6. Abortion: Why all the controversy?

7.   Betrayed
8.   Beyond the Grave: Is there life after death?
9.   Buddy and Rambo: The Orphaned Raccoons
10. Children's Stories II
11. Christ: His Words, His Life
12. Christ: Who is He?
13. Christ's Second Coming: Is it near? How will we know?
14. Coincidences?
15. Death is his Name
16. Do Pets go to Heaven?
17. Evolution: The BIG Lie!
18. Faith: Is faith in God dying?
19. Flesh Wounds of the Mind
20. For the Love of God
21. For the Love of Nature: Four Stories About Birds and Animals
22. God's Holy Days
23. Gun Control: What's the Answer?
24. I'd Rather be Right than Politically Correct
25. Into the West
26. Jerusalem: City of peace?
27. Kenneth Edward Barnes: An autobiography
28. Kenny's Children's Stories
29. Life Along Little Pigeon Creek
30. Loneliness: How to deal with it
31. Madam President
32. Marriage, Infidelity, Divorce: What does the Bible say about it?
33. My Favorite Poems
34. Mysteries of the Bible
35. Mystery of the Antichrist
36. Mystery of the Millennium
37. Odds and Ends: A Collection of Three Stories
38. Outdoor Adventures
39. Plays for Children
40. Ransom
41. Return of the Arkansas River Monster